PUBLIC LIBRARIAN USE OF GOOGLE & ITS FEATURES & APPS

ISBN: 978-1-57440-428-9

Contents

THE QUESTIONNAIRE

CHAPTER 1 – Public Librarian Use of Google and its Apps and Features

1. Please provide the following contact information.

   A. Name:
   B. Organization:
   C. Email Address:
   D. Work Title:
   E. Country

2. What is the approximate Population size of the area served by your library?

3. Age range of survey participant

   A. Under 30
   B. 30-39
   C. 40-49
   D. 50-59
   E. 60-69
   F. 70 or Over

4. Your library's annual budget for all purposes, including salaries, materials, building maintenance, etc. is approximately:

(Please specify the currency if not in US dollars)

5. Your major personal role at the library would best be described as:

   A. reference or information literacy
   B. research or subject specialist
   C. administration
   D. technical services or cataloging
   E. special collections
   F. acquisitions or collection development
   G. Other (please specify)

6. Gender of survey participant

   A. Male

B. Female

CHAPTER 2 – Google

7. What percentage of your total use of search engines would you estimate is accounted for by your use of the Google search engine?

8. How often do you use the following features of Google?

	Never really use it	Seldom use it	Sometimes use it	Often Use it	Very often use it
Google Maps					
Google Advanced Search					
Google Alerts					
Google Notifications					
Google Images					
Google Photos					
Google Calendar					
Chrome					
Google Books					
Google Scholar					
Google Scholar My Citations					
Google Translate					
Google Public Data Explorer					
Google Drive					
Gmail					

Google Earth					
Google Sky					
Google+					
Google Hangouts					
Google Bookmarks					
Google Patent Search					
Google Forms					
Google Slides					
Google Groups					
Google Analytics					
AdWords					
AdSense					
Blogger					
YouTube					

9. When you do use the following features of Google how useful are they to you?

	Don't use this at all	Not very useful	Somewhat useful	Useful	Quite useful	Essential
Google Maps						
Google Advanced Search						
Google Alerts						
Google Notifications						
Google Images						

Google Photos						
Google Calendar						
Chrome						
Google Books						
Google Scholar						
Google Scholar My Citations						
Google Translate						
Google Public Data Explorer						
Google Drive						
Google Earth						
Google Sky						
Google+						
Google Hangouts						
Gmail						
Google Bookmarks						
Google Patent Search						
Google Forms						
Google Slides						
Google Groups						
Google Analytics						

Blogger						
YouTube						

10. For those Google features that you labeled "Quite Useful" or "Essential" what were these features and what do you use them for?

11. Approximately how much time in the past month have you personally spent (in hours or fractions thereof) using the following Google features in connection with your work? If you have not used the feature in the past month put in a zero.

A. Google Maps
B. Google Advanced Search
C. Google Alerts
D. Google Notifications
E. Google Images
F. Google Calendar
G. Chrome
H. Google Books
I. Google Scholar
J. Google Translate
K. Google Public Data Explorer
L. Google Drive
M. Google Earth
N. Google Sky
O. Google+
P. Google Hangouts
Q. Gmail
R. Google Bookmarks
S. Google Patent Search
T. Google Forms
U. Google Slides
V. Google Groups
W. Google Analytics
X. Blogger
Y. YouTube

12. What other apps or features offered by Google but not listed above have you found useful and why?

13. Which single Google app or feature has saved you the most time or made you much more productive?

14. If there was one app or feature in Google that you would like to let your peers know about which one would that be.

PARTICIPANTS LIST

Ada Community Library
Bartram Trail Regional Library System
Blanche K. Werner Public Library
Boyd County Public Library
Brazoria County Library System
Brownell Library
City of Wolfforth Library
Cooke County Library
Coweta Public Library
Dakota City Public Library
Dayton Public Library
Duval County-San Diego Public Library
Fort Vermilion Community Library
Garnavillo Public Library
Gordon City Library
Guymon Public Library & Arts Center
Independence Public Library - Iowa
Iosco-Arenac District Library
Keller Public Library
Keytesville Library
Killeen City Library System
Lake County Library
Le Mars Public Library
Lenox Public Library
Lester Public Library of Vesper
Longview Public Library
M.B. Noelke Jr. Memorial Library
Menlo Public Library
Minersville Public Library
Newbrook Library
Newkirk Public Library
North Central Regional Library
Nueces County Public Libraries
Perry Public Library
Phillips Public Library
Rangeley Public Library
Reinbeck Public Library
Rockwell Public Library
Sioux a Center Public Library
Sunnyvale Public Library
Tyler Public Library
Val Verde County Library
Vista Grande Public Library
Walters Public Library
Waskom Public Library
West Georgia Regional Library
Will Rogers Library

Characteristics of the Sample

Population size of the area served

	#
Less than 2000	14
2000 - 10000	15
10000+ - 45000	15
More than 45000	16
Total	60

Age range of survey participant

	#
Under 30	3
30-39	7
40-49	12
50-59	25
60-69	10
70 or Over	3
Total	60

Library's annual budget $ US

	#
Less than 50000	15
50000 - 300000	16
300000+ - 1500000	15
More than 1500000	14
Total	60

Gender of survey participant

	#
Male	5
Female	55
Total	60

SUMMARY OF MAIN FINDINGS

Characteristics of the Sample

Sixty librarians from public libraries across the United States took part in the "Public Librarian Use of Google & Its Features & Apps" survey. For the survey, the sample was broken out by four sets of criteria: the age and gender of the librarians, the annual budget of the library they work in, and the population size of the areas their libraries serve. First, 55 of the public librarians surveyed are female while just five are male. By age, five are under 30, seven are between 30 and 39, twelve are in the 40-49 age range, twenty-five are in the 50-59 age range, ten are between 60 and 69, and three are 70 or older. By the population size of the area served, fourteen work in libraries that serve populations of less than 2,000, fifteen are from libraries in the 2,000-10,000 population bracket, another fifteen are in the 10,000-45,000 bracket, and sixteen participants are employed by public libraries serving an area with a population of more than 45,000. Finally, fifteen of the public librarians are employees of libraries with annual budgets below $50,000 (USD), sixteen are employees of libraries with annual budgets in the range of $50,000-$300,000, fifteen work in libraries with annual budgets between $300,000 and $1,500,000 and fourteen of the librarians work in libraries with annual budgets above $1,500,000.

Personal Role

We asked the survey participants to describe their major personal role at the library. Of the entire sample, an 80 percent majority said they work in administration, 8.33 percent work in reference or information literacy, 3.33 percent are research or subject specialists, 3.33 percent work in technical services or cataloguing, a further 3.33 percent work in acquisitions or collection development, and just 1.67 percent said they work in special collections.

The results were broken out by the population size of the areas served by the public libraries. In libraries that serve less than 2,000 people, 92.86 percent of the participating librarians work in administration and 7.14 percent work as research or subject specialists. Of the librarians working in libraries that serve 2,000-10,000, 6.67 percent work in acquisitions or collection development while the remaining majority are in administration. In libraries serving an area population of 10,000-45,000, 66.67 percent of the librarians work in administration, 20 percent work in reference or information literacy, and 13.33 percent are in technical services or cataloguing. Finally, of those employed in libraries serving the largest populations, 12.5 percent work in reference or information literacy, 6.25 percent work as research or subject specialists, in special collections, and in acquisitions or collection development, and 68.75 percent have an administrative role.

Search Engine Use

We asked the survey participants, "What percentage of your total use of search engines would you estimate is accounted for by your use of the Google search engine?" Of the entire sample, the percentage of total use of search engines accounted for by the use of the Google search engine was a mean 81.12 percent, the median was 90 percent, and the range was 5 to 100 percent.

The results were broken out by population size of the areas the libraries serve. In libraries that serve less than 2,000, the librarians said a mean 75.50 percent of their search engine use is accounted for by the use of the Google search engine. In libraries which serve more than 45,000 this figure jumps to 85.70 percent. A mean 80.17 percent of search engine use by librarians working in libraries serving area populations of 10,000-45,000 and 83.09 percent of search engine use of those working in libraries serving 2,000-10,000 is accounted for by use of the Google search engine.

The results were further broken out by the age of the survey participants. Librarians between 30 and 39 years old use the Google search engine most often; it accounts for a mean 95.43 percent of their search engine use, in a range of 85-100 percent. At the other end of the spectrum, librarians aged 60-69 years old are the least likely to use the Google search engine; it accounts for just 54.29 percent of their search engine use, in a range of 5 to 95 percent. Across the other age brackets, Google search engine use accounts for a mean 80 percent of search engine use by librarians over 70, 82.4 percent for those aged 50-59, 86.5 percent for those under the age of 30, and Google search engine use accounts for a mean 89.83 percent of all search engine use by librarians aged 40-49.

Google Maps Frequency of Use

The public librarians surveyed shared how often they use Google Maps. Of the entire sample, a 35 percent plurality said they "often use it," 25 percent said they "very often use it," 21.67 percent said they "use it," 15 percent said they "sometimes use it" and just 3.33 percent said they "never really use it."

The results were broken out by the age of the survey participants. Librarians between 50 and 59, and 60 and 65 years of age were the only two groups to say they never really use Google Maps; 4 and 10 percent, respectively, answered thus. A 44 percent plurality of those in the 50-59 age bracket said they often use Google Maps while a 30 percent plurality of the librarians in the 60-69 age bracket said they use it very often. Librarians under the age of 30 use Google Maps the most often; a 66.67 percent majority said they use Google Maps very often while the remaining 33.33 percent said they use it often. In contrast, none of the librarians over the age of 70 said they use Google Maps very often. 33.33 percent of the librarians over the age of 70 surveyed said they use Google Maps "often," "sometimes," and "seldom." Of the librarians between 30 and 39, a 57.14 percent majority said they often use Google Maps, 28.57 percent very often use it, while 14.29 percent said they seldom use Google Maps. Finally, for librarians in the 40-49 age range, 33.33 percent use Google Maps very often and 33.33 percent seldom use it while the remaining 33.33 percent were evenly split between "sometimes" and "often."

Google Advanced Search Frequency of Use

The survey participants shared how often they use Google Advanced Search. Of the entire sample, 15 percent use Google Advanced Search very often, 18.33 percent use it often, 26.67 percent sometimes use it, 28.33 percent seldom use it, 10 percent never really use Google Advanced Search, and the remaining 1.67 percent did not answer the question.

The results were broken out by the population size of the areas served by the libraries. In libraries serving less than 2,000 and in those serving 10,000-45,000, a plurality of librarians seldom use Google Advanced Search; 42.86 and 40 percent respectively answered in this way. In libraries serving populations of 2,000-10,000, the librarians were split, with 33.33 percent saying they sometimes use Google Advanced Search and 33.33 percent saying they often use it. In libraries with more than 45,000 in their service area, a 37.50 plurality of librarians said they use Google Advance Search very often. All librarians working in libraries in this population bracket use this feature; this is the only group for which this is the case. Librarians from libraries in the 2,000-10,000 population bracket were the only group that did not say they use the feature very often.

Google Alerts Frequency of Use

We asked the public librarians how often they use Google Alerts. Of the entire sample, a 55 percent majority said they never really use Google Alerts, 13.33 percent seldom use it, 18.33 percent sometimes use it, 8.33 percent often use it, and 3.33 percent of the librarians said they very often use Google Alerts. The remaining 1.67 percent did not answer the question.

The results were broken out by the population size of the areas served by the public libraries. A majority of all groups said they never really use Google Alerts, except for librarians in libraries serving populations between 2,000 and 10,000; a 40 percent plurality of these librarians said they never use Google Alerts. "Sometimes use it" was the second most commonly given response to the question "How often do you use Google Alerts?" by all librarians except those in libraries serving more than 45,000; 18.75 percent of these librarians said they seldom use it. One of the librarians from a library serving 2,000-10,000 and one from a library serving more than 45,000 said they very often use Google Alerts.

Google Notifications Frequency of Use

We then asked the survey participants how often they use Google Notifications. Of the entire sample, a 51.67 percent majority of the public librarians said they never use Google Notifications, 20 percent seldom use it, 18.33 percent sometimes use it, 6.67 percent often use it, and 3.33 percent very often use them. Once more, the remaining 1.67 percent did not answer the question.

The results were broken out by the population size of the areas the libraries serve. Librarians working in public libraries serving a population size of 2,000-10,000 are the most likely to use Google Notifications; 6.67 percent use it very often, 13.33 percent use it often, and just 33.33 percent said they never use it. Librarians in libraries serving 10,000-

45,000 people were the only other group to say they very often use Google Notifications, 6.67 percent do, while librarians in libraries serving more than 45,000 were the only other group to say they often use Google Notifications, 13.33 percent do. Librarians employed in libraries serving less than 2,000 are the least likely to use Google Notifications; 57.14 percent never use it, 28.57 percent seldom use it, and 14.29 percent sometimes use it.

Google Images Frequency of Use

The survey participants shared how often they use Google Images. Of the entire sample, 8.33 percent never use Google Images, 5 percent seldom use it, 28.33 percent sometimes use it, 31.67 percent often use it, and 26.67 percent very often use this Google feature.

The results were broken out by the age of the librarians. Public librarian use of Google Images decreases with age. Public librarians under the age of 30 use Google Images most often; a 66.67 percent majority of librarians in this youngest age bracket say they use Google Images very often while the remaining 33.33 percent say they use it often. All of the librarians between 30 and 39 use Google Images at least sometimes, 14.29 percent, and a 57.14 percent majority use it very often. For those aged 40-49 years old, 50 percent use it often, 25 percent use it very often, and 8.33 percent use it either sometimes, seldom, or never. A 36 percent plurality of librarians aged 50-59 sometimes use Google Images, 28 percent often use it, 24 percent very often use it, 4 percent seldom use it, and 8 percent never use it. Ten percent of librarians aged 60-69 never use Google Images while another 10 percent only seldom use it. A 40 percent plurality of librarians in the 60-69 age range sometimes use Google Images, 30 percent often use it, and another 10 percent use the feature often. Finally, at the other end of the spectrum, librarians over the age of 70 use Google Images the least often. A 66.67 percent majority of these librarians say they use Google Images "sometimes" while the remaining 33.33 percent never really use it.

The results were further broken out by the size of the population served by the libraries. A 57 percent majority of librarians working in libraries with a service area population of less than 2,000 said they sometimes use Google Images. A 33.33 percent plurality of librarians in the 2,000-10,000 population size bracket said they use Google Images very often. A 33.33 percent plurality of those working in libraries in the next population bracket, 10,000-45,000, said they often use the Google Images feature. Finally, 50 percent of librarians in libraries serving an area with a population of more than 45,000 said they often use Google Images; they were the only group to not say that they never use the feature.

Google Photos Frequency of Use

The public librarians shared how often they use Google Photos. For the entire sample, a 35 percent plurality said they never really use it, 11.67 percent seldom use it, 21.67 percent sometimes use it, 20 percent often use it, and 8.33 percent use the feature very often. The remaining 3.33 percent of the sample did not answer the question.

The results were broken out by the age of librarian. Public librarians between the ages of 30 and 39 use Google Photos most often, a 42.86 percent plurality use Google Photos often and 14.29 percent more use it very often. A 33.33 percent plurality of librarians aged 40-49 and a 44 percent plurality of those aged 50-59 both said they never really use Google

Photos. Librarians under the age of 30 were divided, with 33.33 percent saying they never really use Google Photos, they seldom use it, or the use it very often. A majority of those aged 60-69 years old were also evenly split, with 30 percent saying they never use Google Photos and 30 percent saying they use it often. Finally, a 66.67 percent majority of librarians aged 70 or older sometimes use Google Photos while the remaining 33.33 percent never use it.

The results were further broken out by the library's annual budget. A plurality of all libraries except those with an annual budget below $50,000 said they never really use Google Photos. A 33.33 percent plurality of librarians working in libraries with the lowest annual budgets said they sometimes use Google Photos. Librarians working in libraries with annual budgets between $300,000 and $1,500,000 are the most likely to use Google Photos frequently, 20 percent said they use it often and another 20 percent said they use it very often. Librarians working in public libraries with annual budgets above $1,500,000 were the only participants who did not say they use Google Photos very often.

Google Calendar Frequency of Use

We asked the public librarians, "How often do you use Google Calendar?" Of the entire sample, 41.67 percent said they never really use it, 8.33 percent said they seldom use it, 11.67 percent said they sometimes use it, 6.67 percent said they often use it, and 31.67 percent said they very often use it.

The results were broken out by the size of the populations in the libraries service areas. All of the groups were split between the extremes of never using Google Calendar and using it very often. 42.86 percent of librarians in libraries with a service area population of less than 2,000 never really use Google Calendar while 21.43 percent use it very often. For librarians working in the 2,000-10,000 population bracket, 40 percent never really use Google Calendar and 33.33 percent use it very often. For those employed in libraries in the 10,000-45,000 bracket the split is 33.33/33.33 percent for never and very often. Finally, 50 percent of librarians in libraries serving a population of more than 45,000 never really use Google Calendar while 37.5 percent use it very often.

The results were further broken out by the librarians' gender. A 60 percent majority of male librarians use Google Calendar very often while the remaining 40 percent never use it. Female librarians were more divided in their Google Calendar use; 41.28 percent never really use it, 9.09 percent seldom use it, 12.73 percent sometimes use it, 7.27 percent often use it, and 29.09 percent of female librarians use Google Calendar very often.

Google Chrome Frequency of Use

We asked the public library survey participants about the frequency of use of Google Chrome. Of the entire sample, a 46.67 percent plurality use Google Chrome very often, 18.33 percent often use it, 15 percent sometimes use it, 8.33 percent seldom use it, and 11.67 percent never really use Google Chrome.

The results were broken out by the age of the public librarians. Google Chrome's popularity tends to decrease as the librarian's age increases. A full 100 percent of public librarians under the age of 30 use Google Chrome very often. Of those aged 30-39, 71.43 percent use Google Chrome very often and 14.29 percent use it often while the remainder seldom use it. A 41.67 percent plurality of librarians aged 40-49 use Google Chrome very often and 33.33 percent use it often while a majority of librarians aged 50-59, 56 percent, also use Google Chrome very often and 16 percent use it often. Fifty percent of librarians in the 60-69 year age range only sometimes use Google Chrome, 10 percent use it often, 10 percent use it very often, and 30 percent never use it. Finally, none of the participants over the age of 70 use Google Chrome very often; 33.33 percent never use it, 33.33 percent sometimes use it, and 33.33 percent often use it.

The results were further broken out by the libraries' service area population. While 35.71 percent of librarians in libraries with a service area population of less than 2,000 use Google Chrome very often, none of them said they use it often, and 28.57 percent never use it. 40 percent of librarians in libraries with a service area population of 2,000-10,000 use Google Chrome very often and another 40 percent use it often; 6.67 percent of these librarians use Chrome sometimes, seldom, or never. Librarians working in libraries in the 10,000-45,000 population bracket are more divided; 33.33 percent use Chrome very often, 26.67 percent use it often, 20 percent use it sometimes, 6.67 percent seldom use it, and 13.33 percent never really use it. Finally, librarians working in libraries with service area populations above 45,000 use Google Chrome the most frequently; 75 percent use it very often, 6.25 percent use it often, and the remaining 18.75 percent sometimes use it.

Google Books Frequency of Use

We asked the survey participants, "How often do you use Google Books?" Of the entire sample, 46.67 percent never really use Google Books, 21.67 percent seldom use it, 20 percent sometimes use it, 3.33 percent often use it, and 8.33 percent of the public librarians use Google Books often.

The results were broken out by the age of the survey participants. All of the librarians aged 70 or over never really use Google Books. The librarians at the other end of the age range, below 30 years old, use Google Books most frequently. Sixty-six percent of the youngest librarians use Google Books sometimes while the remaining 33.33 percent use it very often. A majority of librarians between 30 and 39 years old were split between "sometimes" and "often" in describing their Google Book use, 28.57 percent chose each of those answers. A 33.33 percent plurality of librarians aged 40-49 said they never use Google Books but 25 percent said they use it very often. None of the librarians aged 50-59 or 60-69 said they use Google Books very often, or even often. 60 and 50 percent pluralities, respectively, of these two age groups said they never use Google Books.

Google Scholar Frequency of Use

We asked the survey participants about the frequency of their Google Scholar use. Of the entire sample, 63.33 percent never really use it, 16.67 percent said they seldom use it, 8.33 percent said they sometimes use it, 6.67 percent use it often, and 5 percent said they use Google Scholar very often.

The results were broken out by the population size of the areas served by the libraries. Librarians working in libraries with less than 2,000 people in their service area use Google Scholar the least. A 92.86 percent majority of librarians serving the smallest populations never really use Google Scholar and the remaining 7.14 percent seldom use it. A majority of librarians working in libraries serving populations of 2,000-10,000 and in libraries that serve area populations of more than 45,000 also never really use Google Scholar; 60 and 56.25 percent, respectively, do not use the feature. A small 6.67 percent of librarians serving populations of 2,000-10,000 use Google Scholar very often, while 12.5 percent of those serving the largest populations use it very often and another 6.25 percent use Google Scholar often. In libraries serving area populations of 10,000-45,000 a 46.67 percent plurality of librarians never use Google Scholar, 13.33 percent sometimes use it, and 20 percent use it seldom and the same percentage, often.

Google Scholar My Citations Frequency of Use

We then asked the public librarians how often they use Google Scholar My Citations. Of the entire sample, 75 percent never really use Google Scholar My Citations, 15 percent seldom use it, 6.67 percent sometimes use it, 1.67 percent use it often and 1.67 percent use it very often.

Broken out by librarian age, a majority of all groups, except those under the age of 30 and including 100 percent of those over the age of 70 never really use Google Scholar My Citations. A 66.67 percent majority of librarians under the age of 30 said they seldom use Google Scholar My Citations while the remaining 33.33 percent never really use it. Librarians in the 40-49 years of age bracket are the only group to use My Citations often or very often.

The results were further broken out by annual budget numbers. One hundred percent of librarians working in libraries with annual budgets below $50,000 never really use Google Scholar My Citations. The percentages of librarians in the other annual budget brackets that never really use My Citations are: 68.75 percent of those in the $50,000-$300,000 bracket, 60 percent of those in the $300,000-$1,500,000 bracket, and 71.43 percent of those working in libraries with annual budgets above $1,500,000. A librarian in a library with a $50,000-$300,000 annual budget uses My Citations very often while another in a library with a budget of more than $1,500,000 annually uses My Citations often.

Google Translate Frequency of Use

We asked the survey participants, "How often do you use Google Translate?" Of the entire sample, 33.33 percent never really use it, 23.33 percent seldom use it, 30 percent sometimes use it, 10 percent often use it, and just 3.33 percent use Google Translate very often.

The results were broken out by the population size of the areas served by the libraries. In libraries serving populations of less than 2,000 a majority of librarians were split between never and seldom using Google Translate; 42.86 percent chose each of those two responses to describe their Google Translate use. The remaining 14.29 percent of librarians in this population bracket said they sometimes use Google Translate. In libraries serving 2,000-

10,000 the librarians were split 40/40 between never and sometimes using Google translate, while 13.33 percent said they seldom use it and 6.67 percent said they use it very often. A 33.33 percent plurality of librarians working in libraries serving populations of 10,000-45,000 said they seldom use Google translate while 13.33 percent said they use it often and the remaining 53.34 percent were evenly divided between seldom and sometimes using the feature. Finally, a 37.50 percent plurality of librarians working in areas with the largest populations said they sometimes use Google Translate while 25 percent never or often use it, and 6.25 percent seldom or very often use it.

The results were further broken out by the librarians' gender. A 60 percent majority of male librarians said they sometimes use Google Translate. The remaining 40 percent of male librarians were evenly divided in their Google Translate use between never and often using it. A 34.55 percent plurality of female librarians never uses Google Translate while the next highest percentages, 27.27 percent, sometimes use it. 3.64 percent of the female librarians surveyed use Google Translate very often and 9.09 percent often use it.

Google Public Data Explorer Frequency of Use

The public librarians surveyed shared how often they use Google Public Data Explorer. Of the entire sample, 75 percent never really use Public Data Explores, 21.67 percent said they seldom use it, and 3.33 percent sometimes use it.

The results were broken out by the population size of the areas served by the libraries. 31.25 percent of librarians working in libraries serving area populations of more than 45,000, 26.67 percent of those working in libraries with a service area population of 2,000-10,000, 20 percent of those working in libraries with a service area population of 10,000-45,000 and 7.14 percent of librarians working in libraries serving an area population of less than 2,000 said they seldom use Google Public Data Explorer. Public librarians working in libraries with a service area population of 2,000-10,000 were the only group to say they sometimes use Google Public Data Explorer; 13.33 percent do. All the other public librarians never really use this Google feature.

Google Drive Frequency of Use

We asked the survey participants, "How often do you use Google Drive?" Of the entire sample, 41.67 percent never really use Google Drive, 11.67 percent seldom use it, 10 percent sometimes use it, 6.67 percent often use it, and 30 percent use Google Drive very often.

We broke the results out by the libraries annual budgets. Librarians working in libraries with higher annual budgets use Google Drive more often. A 60 percent majority of librarians employed in libraries with an annual budget below $50,000 and a 56.25 percent majority of those working in libraries with annual budgets between $50,000 and $300,000 never really use Google Drive. None of these librarians said they often use the feature. In contrast, a 40 percent plurality of those working in libraries with annual budgets in the $300,000-$1,500,000 range and 42.86 percent of those working in libraries with budgets above $1,500,000 per year said they very often use Google Drive. In addition, 13.33 percent and 14.29 percent, respectively, of librarians in these top two budget brackets said they often use Google Drive.

We further broke the results out by the librarians' ages. Public librarians under the age of 30 are strongly divided in their use of Google Drive, 66.67 percent use it very often while the remaining 33.33 percent never use it. Most librarians in the 30-39 age range favour the feature; a 71.43 percent majority use it very often, while the remaining 28.58 percent were evenly split between using it often and sometimes. Half of the librarians in the 40-49 year age bracket use Google Drive very often while 33.33 percent never really use it; none of these librarians said they use the feature sometimes. There was little agreement among librarians aged 50-59 in terms of Google Drive usage; a 44 percent plurality never really use Google Drive, 16 percent seldom use it, 16 percent sometimes use it, 4 percent often use it, and 20 percent use it very often. For librarians aged 60-69 Google Drive is less appealing; 70 percent never really use the feature and none use it very often. Finally, a 66.67 percent majority of public librarians over the age of 70 never really use Google Drive and the remaining 33.33 percent said they only seldom use it.

Gmail Frequency of Use

Next we asked the public librarian survey participants about the frequency of their Gmail use. Of the entire sample, a 60 percent majority said they use Gmail very often, 16.67 percent use it often, 10 percent sometimes use it, 10 percent seldom use it, and just 3.33 percent said they never really use Gmail.

The results were broken out by the population size of the areas served by the libraries. Librarians working in libraries serving areas with populations between 10,000 and 45,000 were the only group to say they never really use Gmail, 13.33 percent responded thus. A 46 percent plurality of librarians working in this population bracket use Google's email service very often and the next highest percentage, 20 percent, sometimes use it. Librarians working in libraries with a service area population size of 2,000-10,000 use Gmail the most often; 80 percent use it very often and another 13.33 percent use it often. Librarians working in libraries with a service area population size of more than 45,000 have the next highest rating of frequency of Gmail use; 62.50 percent use it very often and 18.75 percent use it often. Finally, 50 percent of librarians employed in libraries serving area populations below 2,000 use Google's email system very often, 21.43 percent use it often, and 14.29 percent either sometimes or seldom use it.

The results were further broken out by the age of the public librarians. All of the librarians under the age of 30 use Gmail very often. Gmail is least popular amongst librarians aged 60-69; 20 percent never really use Gmail while just 20 percent use it very often. The remaining 60 percent of librarians in the 60-69 year age bracket use Gmail sometimes or often. Librarians in the over 70 age range were evenly divided, 33.33 percent use Gmail sometimes, often, and very often. Majorities of librarians in the 30-39, 40-49, and 50-59 age ranges all use Gmail very often but 25 percent of those in the 40-49 age range and 12 percent of those in the 50-59 year age range said they seldom use the email service.

Google Earth Frequency of Use

We asked the survey participants about how frequently they use Google Earth. Of the entire sample, 11.67 percent never really use it, 31.67 percent seldom use it, 28.33 percent sometimes use it, 15 percent often use it, and just 6.67 percent use Google Earth very often. The remaining 6.67 percent did not answer the question.

The results were broken out by the population size of the areas served. A 42.86 percent plurality of librarians working in libraries serving area populations of less than 2,000 sometimes uses Google Earth. None of the librarians in this population bracket said they use Google Earth very often. None of the librarians in the 10,000-45,000 population bracket use Google Earth very often; 33.33 percent sometimes use it and 33.33 percent seldom use it, 26.67 percent often use it, and 6.67 percent never use it. A 40 percent plurality of the librarians working in libraries serving an area population of 2,000-10,000 and a 31.25 percent plurality of those working in libraries serving an area population of more than 45,000 said they seldom use Google Earth. 26.67 percent of librarians in the 2,000-10,000 population size bracket said they sometimes use Google Earth while 0 percent said they never use the feature. A quarter of the librarians working in libraries with service area populations above 45,000 said they never really use Google Earth.

Google Sky Frequency of Use

We then asked the librarians, "How often do you use Google Sky?" Of the entire sample, 65 percent never really use Google Sky, 16.67 percent seldom use it, 10 percent sometimes use it, and 5 percent often use it. The remaining 3.33 percent of the sample did not comment on how often they use Google Sky.

The results were broken out by the ages of the public librarians surveyed. 84 percent of librarians aged 50-59, 66.67 percent of those under the age of 30, 60 percent of those aged 60-69, 57.14 percent of those aged 30-39, 41.67 percent aged 40-49, and 33.33 percent of the librarians aged 70 or over said they never really use Google Sky. Just three groups said they use Google Sky often: 14.29 percent of those in the 30-39 age bracket, 10 percent of those in the 60-69 age bracket, and 4 percent of those in the 50-59 age range. Librarians under the age of 30 are the only group which does not sometimes use Google Sky.

Google+ Frequency of Use

We asked the survey participants, "How often do you use Google+?" Of the entire sample, 56.67 percent said they never really use Google+, 23.33 percent said they seldom use it, 11.67 percent said they sometimes use it, 3.33 percent said they often use it, and 5 percent said they use Google+ very often.

The results were broken out by the population size of the areas served by the libraries. 13.33 percent of librarians working in libraries with service area populations of 10,000-45,000 and 6.67 percent of those working in libraries with service area populations of 2,000-10,000 said they use Google+ very often. 7.14 percent of librarians working in libraries with service area populations of less than 2,000 and 6.25 percent of those working in libraries with service area populations of more than 45,000 said they often use Google+. Librarians working in libraries in the 10,000-45,000 population bracket were the only ones to not have a majority say they never really use Google+; a 46.67 percent plurality of these librarians never really use it while 33.33 percent said they seldom use it.

The results were further broken out by the librarians' ages. 100 percent of librarians under the age of 30 never really use Google+. Only 28.57 percent of librarians aged 30-39 also said they never really use Google+, while 14.29 percent said they use it often and 14.29 percent said they use it very often. Librarians aged 50-59 were the only other group to say they use Google+ often (4 percent) or very often (8 percent). Still, 64 percent of librarians aged 50-59 percent never really use Google+. Of the remaining groups, 50 percent of librarians aged 40-49, 60 percent of those aged 60-69, and just 33.33 percent of librarians 70 or older never really use Google+. The percentages of librarians who use Google+ sometimes are: 4 percent of those aged 50-59, 10 percent of those in the 60-69 age range, 14.29 percent of those in the 30-39 age range, 25 percent of those aged 40-49 and 33.33 percent of those aged 70 or older.

Google Hangouts Frequency of Use

We asked the public librarians, "How often do you use Google Hangouts?" Of the entire sample, 56.67 percent never really use it, 20 percent seldom use it, 11.67 percent sometimes use it, 6.67 percent often use it, and 5 percent use Google Hangouts very often.

The results were broken out by the age of the librarians. All of the librarians under the age of 30 and over the age of 70 that we surveyed said they never use Google Hangouts. The only two groups that use Google Hangout very often are those aged 30-39, 28.57 percent do, and those aged 50-59, 4 percent do. Three groups use Google Hangouts often; 28.57 percent of those in the 30-39 year age range, 8.33 percent of those in the 40-49 year age range, and 4 percent of those in the 50-59 year age range said they use Google Hangouts often.

The results were further broken out by the libraries' annual budgets. A majority of librarians working in libraries with budgets below $50,000 per year and with budgets above $1,500,000 per year never use Google Hangouts; 86.67 percent and 57.14 percent, respectively, do not use the app. Librarians in the $50,000-$300,000 and $300,000-$1,500,000 library annual budget bracket are the only two groups who use Google Hangouts very often; 6.35 percent and 13.33 percent, respectively, said they use the Hangouts very often. 25 percent of librarians working in libraries with annual budgets between $50,000 and $300,000 said they use Google Hangouts often; they were the only group to choose this response when describing their Google Hangout use.

Google Bookmarks Frequency of Use

The survey participants shared how often they use Google Bookmarks. Of the entire sample, 61.67 percent never really use Google Bookmarks, 15 percent seldom use it, 10 percent sometimes use it, 6.67 percent often use it, and another 6.67 percent very often use Google's bookmarking service.

The results were broken out by the populations of the areas the libraries serve. Librarians in libraries serving areas with populations below 2,000 are the least likely to use Google Bookmarks, 71.43 percent never use the service and none said they use it very often or often. While 60 percent of librarians in libraries serving areas with populations between 2,000 and 10,000 never use Google Bookmarks, 20 percent use it very often and 13.33 percent use it often. The only other group to use Bookmarks very often is librarians in the 10,000-45,000 population bracket; 6.67 percent use this Google feature very often and another 6.67 percent use it often. A 46.67 percent plurality of these librarians never really uses Google Bookmarks. A 68.75 percent majority of librarians working in libraries serving areas with populations above 45,000 never use Google Bookmarks but 6.25 percent of these librarians do use the feature often.

Google Patent Search Frequency of Use

We asked the participants about the frequency of their Google Patent Search use. This is one of the least frequently used Google features we asked about. Of the entire sample, 83.33 percent never really use Google Patent Search, 10 percent seldom use it and 6.67 percent sometimes use it.

The results were broken out by the libraries' annual budgets. Librarians working in libraries with the smaller budgets use Google Patent Search more often than librarians working in libraries with larger budgets. 13.33 percent of librarians from libraries with annual budgets below $50,000 and 12.50 percent of librarians from libraries in the $50,000-$300,000 annual budget bracket said they sometimes use Google Patent Search. None of the librarians from the higher budget brackets said they sometimes use Google Patent Search. 26.67 percent of librarians in the $300,000-$1,500,000 library annual budget bracket and 14.29 percent of those in libraries with annual budgets above $1,500,000 said they seldom use the service. All of the other librarians said they never really use Google Patent Search.

Google Forms Frequency of Use

"How often do you use Google Forms?" was the next question asked. Of the entire sample, 50 percent never really use Google Forms, 20 percent seldom use it, 16.67 percent sometimes use it, 8.33 percent often use it, and 3.33 percent often use Google Forms. The remaining 1.67 percent did not answer the question.

The results were broken out by the population size of the areas served by the libraries. The only group of librarians that use Google Forms very often are those working in libraries serving areas with a population size of 2,000-10,000, 13.33 percent of them do. Another 13.33 percent of librarians working in this population bracket use Google Forms often, as do 12.50 percent of those working in libraries that serve an area with a population above 45,000 and 6.67 percent of those working in libraries in the 10,000-45,000 population size bracket. 71.43 percent of librarians employed in libraries serving areas with populations below 2,000, 40 percent of those in libraries serving area populations of 2,000-10,000 and 10,000-45,000, and 50 percent of those working in libraries serving areas with population sizes above 45,000 never really use Google Forms.

The results were further broken out by the librarians' gender. Forty percent of male librarians never really use Google Forms while another 40 percent sometimes do and the remaining 20 percent say they seldom use the online survey creating tool. A majority, 51.91 percent of female librarians do not use Google forms, but 9.09 percent say they use it often and 3.64 percent use it very often.

Google Slides Frequency of Use

Google Slides was the next feature we asked about. Of the entire sample, 66.67 percent never really use Google Slides, 15 percent seldom use it, 13.33 percent sometimes use it, and 1.67 percent often use it. The remaining 3.33 percent of the librarians surveyed did not answer the question.

The greatest variance in responses is seen when the results are broke out by the age of the librarians surveyed. All of the librarians aged 70 or over said they never use Google Slides. At the other end of the spectrum, just 28.57 percent of librarians aged 30-39 said they never use Google Slides while a 57.14 percent majority of these librarians said they sometimes use the software. 66.67 percent of librarians under the age of 30 never really use Google Slides but they were the only group who often use the software, 33.33 percent do. Fifty percent of librarians in the 40-49 and 60-69 age brackets never use Google Slides but 16.67 percent of the younger librarians and 20 percent of the older group sometimes use it. Finally, 88 percent of librarians aged 50-59 never use Google Slides, 8 percent seldom use it and the remaining 4 percent did not answer the question.

Google Groups Frequency of Use

We asked the survey participants, "How often do you use Google Groups?" Of the entire sample, a majority 63.33 percent never really uses Google Groups, 18.33 percent seldom use it, 13.33 percent sometimes us it, 1.67 percent often use it, and another 1.67 percent use it very often. The remaining 1.67 percent did not comment on their use of Google Groups.

The results were broken out by the population size of the areas served by the libraries. Librarians working in libraries with service area populations of 2,000-10,000 are the only librarians who use Google Groups very often while those working in libraries serving 10,000-45,000 are the only ones who use it often. The percentages of librarians who sometimes use Google Groups are: 18.75 percent of those working in libraries with service area populations greater than 45,000, 14.29 percent of those in libraries with service area populations below 2,000, 13.33 percent of those in the 2,000-10,000 populations size bracket, and 6.67 percent of those in the 10,000-45,000 population size bracket.

Google Analytics Frequency of Use

We then asked the public librarians about the frequency of their Google Analytics use. Of the entire sample, 56.67 percent never really use Google Analytics, 16.67 percent sometimes use it, 11.67 percent sometimes use it, 10 percent often use it, and 5 percent use Google Analytics very often.

Again, the results were broken out by the population size of the areas served by the libraries. 6.67 percent of librarians working in libraries serving areas with populations between 10,000 and 45,000 and 12.50 percent of those who work in libraries serving areas with populations above 45,000 use Google Analytics very often. A percentage of all of the groups use Google Analytics often: 7.14 of those in the "less than 2,000" area population bracket, 6.67 percent of those in the 2,000-10,000 and 10,000-45,000 brackets, and 18.67 percent of the public librarians working in libraries that serve areas with populations of more than 45,000. A majority of librarians in the lower two brackets never really use Google Analytics; 85.71 percent for those working in service areas with populations below 2,000 and 73.33 percent for those working in the 2,000-10,000 population bracket never do. A plurality, 37.50 percent, of librarians working in libraries with the largest service area populations also never really use Google Analytics while a plurality, 46.67 percent, of those working in service areas with populations of 10,000-45,000 said they seldom use the feature.

AdWords Frequency of Use

"How often do you use AdWords?" was the next question. Of the entire sample, 86.67 percent never really use it, 8.33 percent seldom use it, and 1.67 percent sometimes use it. The remaining 3.33 percent did not answer the question.

The results were broken out by the libraries' annual budgets. A librarian working in a library with an annual budget between $50,000 and $300,000 was the only participant who sometimes uses Google AdWords. By budget, the percentages of librarians who never use AdWords are: 86.67 percent of those in libraries with budgets below $50,000 per year, 87.50 percent of those working in the $50,000-$300,000 budget bracket, 86.67 percent of those in the $300,000-$1,500,000 bracket, and 85.71 percent of those working in libraries with budgets above $1,500,000 per year.

AdSense Frequency of Use

We asked the participants how often they use AdSense. This is a very infrequently used Google feature. Of the entire sample, 88.33 percent said they never really use AdSense, 10 percent said they seldom use it, and just 1.67 percent said they sometimes use it. Broken out across all subgroups a female librarian, aged 40-49, employed in a library with an annual budget between $50,000 and $300,000 and serving an area population of 2,000-10,000 was the only participant who sometimes uses Google AdWords.

The results were further broken out by population size of the area served. The percentages of librarians in each population bracket indicating that they seldom use Google AdWords are: 6.67 percent of those in the 2,000-10,000 service area population range, 7.14 percent of those in libraries with service area populations below 2,000, 12.50 percent of those in libraries with service area populations above 45,000, and 13.33 percent of those in the 10,000-45,000 area population size bracket.

Blogger Frequency of Use

Blogger was the next Google feature we asked about. Of the entire sample, 76.67 percent said they never really use Blogger, 11.67 percent said they seldom use it, 5 percent said they sometimes use it, 1.67 percent said they use it often and 3.33 percent said they use Blogger very often. The remaining 1.67 percent did not answer the question.

The results were broken out by the age of the librarians. Two groups use Blogger very often: 33.33 percent of librarians under the age of 30 and 8.33 percent of those aged 40-49. Librarians aged 40-49 were also the only group to say they use Blogger often, 8.33 percent do. By age, the percentages of librarians who do not use Blogger are: 33.33 percent of those under 30, 41.67 percent of those aged 40-49, 66.67 percent of those 70 years of age or older, 71.43 percent of those aged 30-39, 80 percent of those aged 60-69, and a full 100 percent of librarians aged 50-59.

The results were further broken out by gender. All of the male librarians we surveyed they really use Blogger. 74.55 percent of female librarians also never really use Blogger while 12.73 percent seldom use it, 5.45 percent sometimes use it, 1.82 percent often use it, and 3.64 percent use Blogger very often.

YouTube Frequency of Use

We asked the survey participants, "How often do you use YouTube?" Of the entire sample, 10 percent never really use YouTube, 18.33 percent said they seldom use it, 31.67 percent sometimes use it, 25 percent use it often, and 15 percent use it very often.

The results were broken out by the population size of the areas served by the libraries. All of the librarians from libraries with service area populations greater than 45,000 use YouTube; a 37.50 percent plurality of them use it often and another 18.75 percent use it very often. The service area population bracket with the highest percentage of librarians who never use YouTube is the 10,000-45,000 bracket; 20 percent of these librarians never use YouTube. A 26.67 percent plurality of librarians serving area population of 10,000-45,000 sometime uses YouTube. A 46.67 percent plurality of librarians working in libraries that serve areas with populations of 2,000-10,000 also only sometimes use YouTube; 13.33 percent of these librarians chose each of the remaining answers to describe the frequency of their YouTube use. Finally, a 35.71 percent plurality of librarians working in libraries with service area populations below 2,000 said they seldom use YouTube but the next highest percent, 28.57 percent, said they often use YouTube.

The results were further broken out by the age of the survey participants. Librarians aged 40-49 and those aged 60-69 are the only groups with members who never use YouTube; 33.33 and 20 percent, respectively, said they never use the feature. Librarians aged 70 or older were the only group who do not use YouTube very often or even often; 66.67 percent said they seldom use it and the remaining 33.33 percent only use it sometimes. A 44 percent plurality of librarians aged 50-59 and a 30 percent plurality of those aged 60-69 said they only sometimes use YouTube. A 42.86 percent plurality of librarians aged 30-39 use YouTube often. The youngest librarians surveyed, those under the age of thirty, were evenly divided in the frequency of their YouTube use between seldom, often, and very often.

Usefulness of Google Maps

Our next series of questions focused on the usefulness (as opposed to the frequency of use) of various Google features and Apps. Some features and apps may be used infrequently but may be highly valued when they are used. We began by asking, "When you do use Google Maps how useful is it to you?" Of the entire sample, 10 percent said Google Maps are not very useful, 15 percent said they are somewhat useful, 38.33 percent said they are useful, 33.33 percent said they are quite useful, and the remaining 3.33 percent said they do not use Google Maps.

The results were broken out by the population size of the areas served by the libraries. 21.43 percent of librarians from libraries with the smallest service area populations, 6.67 percent of those from libraries with service area populations between 2,000 and 10,000, and 13.33 percent of those from libraries with service area populations between 10,000 and 45,000 said they do not find Google Maps to be very useful when they do use them. A 40 percent plurality of librarians from libraries with service area populations in the 2,000-10,000 range and a 46.67 percent plurality of those from libraries with service area populations in the 10,000-45,000 range said they find Google Maps to be quite useful. Half of the librarians in libraries with less than 2,000 people in their library's service area and a 43.75 percent plurality of those with more than 45,000 people in their library's service area said Google Maps are useful.

Usefulness of Google Advance Search

The survey participants shared how useful they find Google Advanced Search to be, when they use the feature. Of the entire sample, 1.67 percent said Google Advanced Search is not very useful, 16.67 percent find it somewhat useful, 16.67 percent find it useful, 25 percent find it quite useful, and 11.67 percent said Google Advanced Search is essential. The remaining 23.88 percent said they do not use Google Advanced Search.

The results were broken out by the age of the survey participants. All of the librarians under the age of 30 use Google Advanced Search, they are evenly divided in their estimation of the features usefulness between somewhat useful, quite useful, and essential. Of the more than 85 percent of librarians aged 30-39 who use Google Advanced Search, a 42.86 percent plurality find it quite useful and 28.57 percent find it essential. Three quarters of the librarians aged 40-49 use Google Advanced Search and a 33.33 percent plurality of them find it useful. For the 64 percent of librarians aged 50-59 who use Google Advanced Search, 20 percent find it somewhat useful, 20 percent find it quite useful, 16 percent find it useful, and 8 percent find it essential. Librarians aged 60-69 were the only group to say they do not find Google Advanced Search to be very useful, 10 percent answered thus. A 30 percent plurality of librarians aged 60-69 said Google Advanced Search is quite useful. Finally, the 33.33 percent of librarians aged 70 or older who use Google Advanced Search said they find the feature to be useful.

Usefulness of Google Alerts

We asked the public librarians to share how useful Google Alerts are to them. Of the entire sample, 3.33 percent said Google Alerts are not very useful, 10 percent said they are somewhat useful, 20 percent said they are useful, 8.33 percent said they are quite useful, and 1.67 percent said Google Alerts are essential to them. A little more than half of the participants said they do not use Google Alerts and 5 percent did not answer the question.

The results were broken out by the libraries' annual budgets. Librarians from the lowest and highest annual budget brackets were the only two groups to say they do not find Google Alerts to be very useful; 6.67 percent from libraries with annual budgets below $50,000 and 7.14 percent from libraries with budgets above $1,500,000 per year answered thus. Another 7.14 percent of librarians working in libraries in the highest budget bracket and 6.67 percent of those in the lowest budget bracket, as well as 20 percent of librarians working in libraries with annual budgets between $300,000 and $1,500,000 said they find Google Alerts to be quite useful. A librarian from a library with a $300,000-$1,500,000 annual budget was the only participant to say Google Alerts is essential to them.

The results were further broken out by gender. Of the 60 percent of male librarians surveyed who use Google Alerts, 20 percent said they are not very useful, 20 percent said they are somewhat useful, and 20 percent said they are quite useful. 41.82 percent of female participants use Google Alerts and answered the question; a shade more than half of these, or 21.82 percent of all survey participants find Google Alerts to be useful, 9.09 percent said Alerts are somewhat useful, 7.27 percent said the feature is quite useful, 1.82 percent said it is essential, and 1.82 percent said they do not find Google Alerts to be useful at all.

Usefulness of Google Notifications

Next we asked about Google Notifications. Of the entire sample, 6.67 percent said the feature is not very useful, 13.33 percent said it is somewhat useful, 16.67 percent said it is useful, 5 percent said it is quite useful, and another 5 percent said they find Google Notifications to be an essential feature. More than half of the participants, 51.67 percent, said they do not use Google Notifications and 1.67 percent did not comment on the usefulness of Notifications.

The results were broken out by the population size of the areas served by the libraries. Of the librarians working in service areas with populations under 2,000, 7.14 said they find Google Notifications to not be very useful and 7.14 percent said the feature is only somewhat useful to them. Librarians in the 2,000-10,000 population bracket were a little more positive about Google Notifications' usefulness; 13.33 percent said the feature is somewhat useful, 33.33 percent said it is useful, 6.67 percent said it is quite useful, and another 6.67 percent said they find the service to be essential. The 40 percent of librarians working in libraries with service area populations of 10,000-45,000 are evenly divided in their estimations of Google Notifications usefulness between not very useful, useful, and essential in their estimations of Google Notifications usefulness. Librarians working in libraries with service area populations greater than 45,000 are the most likely to use Google Notifications, and the most divided in their estimates of the service's usefulness; 6.25 percent said it is not very useful, 31.25 percent said it is somewhat useful, 18.75 think it is useful, and 12.50 percent said it is quite useful.

Usefulness Google Images

We asked the survey participants how useful they consider Google Images to be. Of the entire sample, a 36.67 percent plurality said they find Google Images quite useful, 26.67 percent considered the feature essential, 18.33 percent said it is useful, and 8.33 percent thought it is somewhat useful. The remaining 10 percent did not use Google Images.

The results were broken out by the age of the librarians surveyed. All of the librarians under the age of 40 use Google Images. Librarians under the age of 30 find the feature to be the most useful when they use it, 66.67 percent said it is essential while the remaining 33.33 percent said it is quite useful. A 57.14 percent majority of librarians aged 30-39 also find Google Images to be quite useful while the rest say the feature is essential. A 66.66 percent majority of librarians aged 40-49 were evenly divided between "quite useful" and "essential" in their description of Google Images' usefulness and the remaining 25 percent who use the feature said it is useful. For a plurality of librarians aged 50-59 Google Images is quite useful while the next highest percentage simply finds it useful. Of the 70 percent of librarians aged 60-69 who use Google Images, 20 percent rate it either "somewhat useful," "quite useful," or "essential," and 10 percent said it is useful. Finally, 33.33 percent of librarians 70 years of age or older do not use Google Images, 33.33 percent do use it and find it somewhat useful, and 33.33 percent use it and find it useful.

The results were further broken out by the libraries' annual budgets. 26.67 percent of librarians working in libraries with an annual budget below $50,000 and 12.50 percent of those working in libraries with an annual budget of $50,000-$300,000 do not use Google Images. The percentages of librarians who use Google Images and find it to be essential are: 13.33 percent of librarians working in libraries with an annual budget below $50,000, 31.25 percent of those in the $50,000-$300,000 library annual budget bracket, 26.67 percent of those in the $300,000-$1,500,000 budget bracket, and 35.71 percent of librarians working in libraries with an annual budget above $1,500,000. At the other end of the spectrum, the percentages of librarians who use Google Images and find it to be only somewhat useful are: 6.67 percent of librarians in the lowest annual budget bracket, 6.25 percent of those in the $50,000-$300,000 library annual budget bracket, 13.33percent of those in the $300,000-$1,500,000 budget bracket, and 7.14 percent of librarians working in libraries with annual budgets above $1,500,000.

Usefulness of Google Photos

We asked the public librarians: how useful is Google Photos? Of the entire sample, 8.33 percent said Google Photos is not very useful, 13.33 percent said it is somewhat useful, 15 percent said it is useful, 18.33 percent said it is quite useful, and 6.67 percent said it is essential. 35 percent of the participants said they do not use Google Photos and 3.33 percent did not comment on the usefulness of the feature.

The results were broken out by the population size of the areas served by the libraries. None of the librarians employed in libraries serving areas with populations of less than 2,000 or more than 45,000 said they find Google Photos to be essential. In contrast, 6.67 percent of librarians employed in the 2,000-10,000 population bracket and 20 percent of those in the 10,000-45,000 population bracket do find this feature to be essential. Librarians working in libraries with a service area population of 2,000-10,000 are the only librarians who do not find Google Images to be not very useful; a 33.33 percent plurality of these librarians find the feature quite useful. Of the librarians who do use Google Photos, a 21.43 percent plurality of those working in areas with the smallest populations and a 18.75 percent plurality of those working in areas with the largest populations also find Google Photos to be quite useful. None of the librarians working in libraries with a service area population between 10,000 and 45,000 find Google Photos to be quite useful, a 26.67 percent plurality of these librarians who use the feature only consider it to be somewhat useful.

Usefulness of Google Calendar

We then asked the participants, "When you use Google Calendar, how useful is it to you?" Of the entire sample, 6.67 percent said Google Calendar is not very useful, 5 percent said it is somewhat useful, 13.33 percent said it is useful, 11.67 percent said it is quite useful, and 30 percent said it is essential. 31.67 percent of the librarians said they do not use Google Calendar and the remaining 1.67 percent did not comment on the usefulness of the feature.

The results were broken out by the population size of the areas served by the libraries. Most of the librarians who do use Google Calendar find it to be quite useful or essential. None of the librarians working in libraries with a service area population between 2,000 and 10,000 said they found Google Calendar to be anything less than useful. A small percentage of each group of librarians said they think Google Calendar is not very useful or only somewhat useful. 7.14 of librarians working in libraries serving area populations of less than 2,000 said Google Calendar was not very useful and another said it was just somewhat useful, 13.33 and 6.67 percent of librarians in the 10,000-45,000 population bracket said the feature is not very and somewhat useful, and 6.25 percent of librarians working in libraries serving areas with populations greater than 45,000 said Google Calendar is not very useful and somewhat useful.

The results were further broken out by the librarians' gender. 40 percent of male librarians do not use Google Calendar compared to 30.91 percent of female librarians. 40 percent of the male librarians find Google Calendar to be essential and another 20 percent find it quite useful. None of the male librarians said Google Calendar is not very useful. Of the female librarians, 29.09 percent said Google Calendar is essential and 10.91 percent said it is quite useful, while 7.27 percent said it is not very useful at all.

Usefulness of Chrome

Next, the survey participants shared how useful they find Google Chrome to be when they use the browser. Most of the librarians find Google Chrome to be very useful. Of the entire sample, a 38.33 percent majority said they think Google Chrome is essential, 25 said it is quite useful, 16.67 percent said it is useful, 1.67 percent said it is somewhat useful, and 5 percent said they do not find Google Chrome to be useful. 11.67 percent of the public librarians said they do not use Google's Chrome browser and 1.67 percent did not answer the question.

The results were broken out by the age of the survey participants. The percentages of public librarians who use Google Chrome but find it to be not very useful are: 14.29 percent of librarians aged 30-39, 4 percent of those aged 50-59 and 10 percent of those aged 60-69. Ten percent of librarians aged 60-69 also said they find Google Chrome to be only somewhat useful, they were the only group who used this phrase to describe the browser's usefulness. All of the librarians under the age of 30 that we surveyed said Google Chrome is essential to them. None of the librarians over the age of 70 think Google Chrome is essential; they were the only group who did not rate Chrome essential. The 66.66 percent of the librarians aged 70 or older who use Chrome said it is simply useful.

The results were further broken out by the population size of the areas served by the libraries. All of the librarians who work in libraries that serve areas with populations over 45,000 use Google Chrome and a vast majority find the browser to be especially useful; 50 percent said it is essential and 43.75 percent said it is quite useful while just 6.25 percent said it is simply useful. A plurality of both librarians working in libraries serving area populations of 2,000-10,000 and 10,000-45,000 also said they find Google Chrome to be essential. A 35.71 percent plurality of librarians working in libraries that serve the least populated areas do not use Google Chrome but when librarians in this group do use the browser 21.43 percent find it useful, 21.43 percent find it quite useful, and 14.29 percent find it essential.

Usefulness of Google Books

Next we asked about the usefulness of Google Books. Of the entire sample, when they use Google Books 3.33 percent find the service to not be very useful, 15 percent said it is somewhat useful, 16.67 percent said it is useful, 8.33 percent said it is quite useful, and another 8.33 percent said they find Google Books to be essential. A 46.67 percent plurality of the public librarians said they do not use this service at all and 1.67 percent did not answer the question.

The results were broken out by the libraries' annual budgets. The only librarians to say they do not find Google Books to be very useful at all were those working in a library with an annual budget between $300,000 and $1,500,000, 13.33 percent answered thus. The only group to not consider Google Books essential was librarians working in libraries with annual budgets below $50,000. Of the other budget brackets, 6.25 percent in the $50,000-$300,000 bracket, 6.67 percent of those in the $300,000-$1,500,000 bracket, and 21.43 percent of those in the "more than $1,500,000" bracket all said Google Books is essential.

The results were further broken out by the age of the librarians. 100 percent of librarians aged 70 or over said they do not use Google Books. In contrast, 100 percent of librarians under the age of 30 do use Google Books and a 66.67 percent plurality of them find the service essential while the remaining 33.33 percent describe it as being "quite useful." Librarians aged 40-49 were the only other group to rate Google Books essential, 25 percent did. This group was also one two to say that Google Books is not very useful; 8.33 percent do not find it to be a very useful service nor do 10 percent of librarians aged 60-69. The other 40 percent of librarians aged 60-69 who use Google Books were evenly divided between "somewhat useful" and "useful" in their estimation of the service's usefulness. Of the 71.43 percent of librarians aged 30-39 who use Google Books and commented on the service's usefulness, 28.57 find it somewhat useful, 14.29 percent find it useful, and another 28.57 percent find it quite useful. Finally, 20 percent of librarians aged 60-69 said

Google Books is somewhat useful, 26 percent said it is useful, and 4 percent said they think it is quite useful.

Usefulness of Google Scholar

We asked the survey participants, "When you do use Google Scholar, how useful is it to you?" Of the entire sample, 3.33 percent said it is not very useful, 5 percent said it is somewhat useful, 11.67 percent said it is useful, 5 percent said it is quite useful, and 10 percent said it is essential. 65 percent of the public librarians said they do not use Google Scholar.

The results were broken out by the population size of the areas served by the libraries. Librarians working in libraries with service area populations in the 2,000-10,000 and the 10,000-45,000 ranges were the only groups who do not find Google Scholar to be very useful when they use the feature, 6.67 percent of both groups responded thus. At the other end of the spectrum, 6.67 percent of librarians working in libraries in the 2,000-10,000 area population bracket, 13.33 percent of those in the 10,000-45,000 bracket, and 18.75 percent of those employed in libraries with service area populations above 45,000 said they find Google Scholar to be an essential feature. The 7.14 percent of librarians working in libraries with a service area population of less than 2,000 who do use Google Scholar said the feature is just somewhat useful.

The results were further broken out by gender. Of the 60 percent of male librarians who use Google Scholar, 40 percent find the feature to be quite useful and 20 percent said it is essential. The female librarians were slightly less positive in their opinions of Google Scholars' usefulness. Of the 32.73 percent of female librarians who use Google Scholar, 3.64 percent said it is not very useful, 5.45 percent said it is somewhat useful, 12.73 percent said it is useful, just 1.82 percent said it is quite useful, and 9.09 percent said it is essential.

Usefulness of Google Scholar My Citations

We asked the survey participants how useful Google Scholar My Citations is to them, when they use the feature. Of the entire sample, 3.33 percent said they do not consider Google Scholar My Citations to be very useful, 6.67 percent said it is somewhat useful, 8.33 said it is useful, 3.33 percent said it is quite useful, and 1.67 percent said they think My Citations is essential. Three quarters of the participants said they do not use Google Scholar My Citations and 1.67 percent of the sample did not answer the question.

The results were broken out by the libraries' annual budgets. All of the librarians working in libraries with annual budgets below $50,000 said they do not use Google Scholar My Citations. Of the 31.25 percent of librarians working in libraries with annual budgets between $50,000 and $30,000, a 12.50 percent plurality said they find Google Scholar to be useful, while 6.25 percent each said it is not very useful, somewhat useful, and essential. A plurality of librarians who use Google Scholar My Citations and who work in libraries with annual budgets of $300,000-$1,500,000 also said they find the feature to be useful, 20 percent out of 46.67 percent responded thus. None of these librarians said they find My Citations to be quite useful or essential. Finally, of the 21.43 percent of librarians working in libraries with budgets above $1,500,000 per year who do use Google Scholar My Citations, 14.29 percent said it is quite useful and 7.14 percent said it is somewhat useful.

Usefulness of Google Translate

Next we asked about Google Translate. Of the entire sample, 1.67 percent said Google Translate is not very useful, 18.33 percent said it is somewhat useful, 21.67 percent said it is useful, 16.67 percent said it is quite useful, and 8.33 percent said it is essential. The remaining one third of the participants said they do not use Google Translate.

The results were broken out by the population size of the areas served by the libraries. Librarians working in libraries that serve areas with populations greater than 45,000 find Google Translate to be the most useful, 25 percent said it is essential, 12.50 percent said it is quite useful, and 31.25 percent said it is useful. That said they were also the only group to say that Google Translate is not very useful. Librarians working in libraries serving areas with populations of less than 2,000 had the lowest opinion of googles usefulness; 35.71 percent said it is only somewhat useful and none of the librarians said it was either quite useful or essential. Of the librarians who work in libraries serving area populations of 2,000-10,000, a 26.67 percent plurality said they find Google Translate to be useful while the next highest percentage, 20 percent, said it is quite useful. They were the only other group to rate Google Translate's usefulness "essential," 6.67 percent did. A 33.33 percent plurality of librarians working in libraries serving area populations of 10,000-45,000 said they think Google Translate is quite useful; they were followed by 26.67 percent who find it just somewhat useful.

The results were further broken out by the age of the survey participants. There was little agreement amongst the different age groups in their opinion of Google Translate's usefulness. Of the two thirds of librarians under the age of the 30 who use Google Translate, 33.33 percent think it is quite useful and 33.33 percent think it is essential. In contrast, of the two thirds of librarians aged 70 or older who use Google Translate, 33.33 percent think it is somewhat useful and the other 33.33 percent think it is simply useful. A 42.86 percent plurality of librarians aged 30-39 think Google Translate is quite useful, a 30 percent plurality of those aged 60-69 think it is somewhat useful, and 50 percent of the librarians aged 40-49 were split evenly between useful and essential in their opinion of Google Translate's usefulness.

Usefulness of Google Data Explorer

We asked the survey participants, "When you do use Google Public Data Explorer, how useful is it to you?" Of the entire sample, 6.67 percent said Google Public Data Explorer is not very useful to them, 8.33 percent said it is somewhat useful, and 10 percent said it is useful. 73.33 percent of the public librarians said they do not use Google Public Data Explorer and 1.67 percent did not comment on the useful product.

The results were broken out by the population size of the areas served by the libraries. 100 percent of the librarians working in libraries with service area populations of less than 2,000 do not use Google Public Data Explorer. Librarians working in libraries with service area populations of more than 45,000 are the most likely to use Public Data Explorer, 56.25

percent said they do not and 6.25 percent did not answer the question. Of the librarians in the largest population bracket who do use it, 18.75 percent said it is useful and 12.5 percent said it is somewhat useful. Of the 33.33 percent of librarians working in service areas with populations of 2,000-10,000 who use Google Public Data Explorer, 20 percent think it is useful and 13.33 percent think it is not very useful. Just 26.67 percent of librarians working in libraries with a service area population of 10,000-45,000 use Google Public Data; 20 percent said it is just somewhat useful while the remaining 6.67 percent said it is not very useful.

Usefulness of Google Drive

We asked the survey participants to rate the usefulness of Google Drive. Of the entire sample, 10 percent said when they use Google Drive they do not find it to be very useful, 6.67 percent said they find it somewhat useful, 6.67 percent said it is useful, 13.33 percent said it is quite useful, and 25 percent said they find Google Drive to be essential. The remaining 38.33 percent of the participants said they do not use Google Drive.

The results were broken out by the population size of the areas served by the libraries. The percentages of librarians who use Google Drive and consider the feature to be essential are: 7.14 percent of librarians working in libraries with service area populations of less than 2,000, 26.67 percent of those working in libraries with service area populations between 2,000 and 10,000, 33.33 percent of those working in libraries with service area populations of 10,000-45,000, and 31.25 percent of those working in libraries with service area populations of more than 45,000. At the other end of the spectrum, 7.14 percent of librarians employed in the lowest service area population bracket, 20 percent of those in the 2,000-10,000 population bracket, and 13.33 percent of the librarians working in libraries with a service area population of 10,000-45,000 said they find Google Drive to not be very useful.

The results were further broken out by the age of the librarians surveyed. All of the librarians aged 30-39 use Google Drive and they find it very useful, 57.14 percent said it is essential while the remaining 42.86 percent said it is quite useful. The 66.67 percent of librarians under the age of 30 who use Google Drive all consider the program to be essential. A plurality, 41.67 percent of librarians aged 40-49 also think Google Drive is essential, while the remaining 33.34 percent who use it think it is either quite useful or useful. There was less agreement among librarians aged 50-59 as to the usefulness of Google Drive; 8 percent said it is not very useful, 16 percent said it is somewhat useful, 8 percent said it is useful, 4 percent said it is quite useful, and another 16 percent said it is essential. Just 33.33 percent of librarians aged 70 or older use Google Drive and all of them said it is not very useful.

Usefulness of Google Earth

We asked the survey participants, "When you do use Google Earth, how useful is it to you?" The participants find Google Earth to be a useful tool. Of the entire sample, just 5 percent said Google Earth is not very useful, 23.33 percent said it is somewhat useful, 30 percent said it is useful, 10 percent said it is quite useful, and 10 percent said they find Google Earth to be essential. The remaining 21.67 percent of the public librarians surveyed said they do not use Google Earth.

The results were broken out by the population size of the areas served by the libraries. A plurality, 35.71 percent of librarians working in libraries serving areas with populations below 2,000 said when they use Google Earth it is useful to them but they were the only group who did not have at least some members who believe that Google Earth is essential. A 46.67 percent plurality of librarians working in libraries with service area populations between 2,000 and 10,000 also said Google Earth is useful and 20 percent said it is essential. Of the librarians working in libraries serving areas with populations in the 10,000-45,000 range, a 33.33 percent plurality said Google Earth is somewhat useful, 20 percent said it is useful, 20 percent said it is quite useful, 6.67 percent said it is essential and another 6.67 percent said it is not very useful. A 25 percent plurality of librarians working in libraries serving area populations greater than 45,000 also said they find Google Earth to be just somewhat useful; they were the only group who did not say Google Earth was not very useful and 12.5 percent said it is essential.

The results were further broken out by the age of the librarians participating in the survey. All 33.33 percent of librarians under the age of 30 who use Google Earth said it is essential while all 66.67 percent of librarians aged 70 or older who use the feature said it is simply useful. Librarians aged 30-39 find Google Earth the most useful, 42.86 percent described it as being quite useful and 14.29 percent said it is essential while none described it as being not very useful. In contrast librarians aged 60-69 find Google Earth to be the least useful; 20 percent said it is not very useful, 30 percent said it is somewhat useful, and 10 percent said it is useful, quite useful, and essential. The only other group to say Google Earth is not very useful was librarians between 40 and 49, 8.33 percent answered thus, while another 8.33 percent said it is essential and a 41.67 percent plurality said it is useful. A 36 percent plurality of librarians aged 50-59 also said Google Earth is useful to them.

Usefulness of Google Sky

Next we asked the survey participants to comment on the usefulness of Google Sky. Most of the public librarians do not use the feature, 63.33 percent, and 6.67 percent did not answer the question. Of the entire sample, 3.33 percent said Google Sky is not very useful to them, 11.67 percent said it is somewhat useful, 6.67 percent said it is useful, 6.67 percent said it is quite useful, and just 1.67 percent said Google Sky is essential.

The results were again broken out by the population size of the areas served by the libraries. The only group who said Google Sky, when they use the feature, is essential to them was librarians working in libraries serving area populations of more than 45,000. At the other end of the spectrum, 6.67 percent of both librarians working in libraries with service area populations of 2,000-10,000 and 10,000-45,000 said they do not find Google Sky to be very useful at all. Librarians working in libraries serving populations of less than 2,000 were split between “somewhat useful” and “quite useful” in their estimations of Google Sky’s usefulness. A 20 percent plurality of librarians in the 2,000-10,000 population size bracket who do use Google Sky said it is useful. Of those librarians in the 10,000-45,000 and “more than 45,000” population brackets who do use Google Sky, pluralities said the feature is just somewhat useful.

Usefulness of Google+

The survey participants next commented on the usefulness of Google+. Of the entire sample, 10 percent said when they use Google+ it is not very useful to them, 16.67 percent said it is somewhat useful, 5 percent said it is useful, 6.67 percent said it is quite useful, and 3.33 percent said Google+ is essential to them. A 56.67 percent majority of the sample said they do not use Google+ and 1.67 percent did not provide an answer to the question.

The results were broken out by the libraries' annual budgets. Those who find Google+ the most useful are librarians working in libraries with annual budgets in the $50,000-$300,000 and $300,000-$1,500,000 ranges, 6.67 percent of both said Google+ is essential to them. 13.33 percent of librarians working in libraries with budgets below $50,000 per year, a plurality of those who do use Google+, said they find the feature to be quite useful. Pluralities of librarians who work in libraries with annual budgets in the $50,000-$300,000 range and more than $1,500,000 who do use Google+ said they find the feature to be somewhat useful. A 20 percent plurality of librarians who do use Google+ and who work in libraries with budgets between $300,000 and $1,500,000 per year said they do not find the feature to be very useful at all. 12.5 percent of librarians working in libraries in the $50,000-$300,000 budget range, and 7.14 percent of those working in libraries with annual budgets greater than $1,500,000 also said they find Google+ to be not very useful at all.

The results were further broken out by Gender. 60 percent of male librarians surveyed do not use Google+, the remaining 40 percent are equally divided between "not very useful" and "quite useful" in their opinion of the feature's usefulness. Of the female librarians, 5636 percent do not use Google+, 18.18 percent do use it and find it somewhat useful, 9.09 percent do not think it is very useful at all, 5.45 percent said it is useful, another 5.45 percent said it is quite useful, and 3.64 percent said Google+ is essential. The remaining 1.82 percent of female librarians surveyed did not comment of Google+'s usefulness.

Usefulness of Google Hangouts

We asked the public librarians about the usefulness of Google Hangouts. Again, most of the participants, 51.67 percent, do not use Google Hangouts; those who do are quite divided in their opinions of its usefulness. Of the entire sample, 3.33 percent said when they do use Google Hangouts it is not very useful to them, 16.67 percent said it is somewhat useful, 10 percent said it is useful, 8.33 percent said it is quite useful, and 5 percent said it is essential. 5 percent of the participants did not comment on Google Hangouts' usefulness.

The results were broken out by the population size of the areas served by the libraries. Of those who had very favourable opinions about Google Hangouts' usefulness, 7.14 percent of librarians working in libraries serving areas with populations of less than 2,000 and 13.33 percent serving area populations of 2,000-10,000 said Google Hangouts is essential while 20 percent of librarians working in libraries serving area populations of 10,000-45,000 and 12.50 percent of those working in libraries with service area populations of more than 45,000 said Google Hangouts is quite useful. The only group to say Google Hangouts is not very useful at all were librarians working in the 10,000-45,000 service area population bracket, 13.33 percent of these librarians do not find Google Hangouts to be very useful.

Usefulness of Gmail

Next we asked the participants, "When you do use Gmail, how useful is it to you?" According to the public librarians surveyed, Gmail is Google's most useful feature. Of the entire sample, a 56.67 percent majority said Gmail is essential, 13.33 percent said it is quite useful, 10 percent said it is useful, and 13.33 percent said it is somewhat useful. Just 5 percent of the librarians said they do not use Gmail, and 1.67 percent did not answer the question.

The results were broken out by the population size of the areas served by the libraries. A majority of all the groups, except those in the lowest area population size bracket said they find Gmail to be essential. Just 21.43 percent of librarians working in libraries with a service area population below 2,000 said Gmail is essential, a 35.71 percent plurality said it is quite useful. The percentages who find Gmail to be only somewhat useful are: 21.43 percent of librarians working in service areas with populations under 2,000, 6.67 percent of those working in libraries serving areas with populations in the 2,000-10,000 range, 13.33 percent of those working in libraries serving populations of 10,000-45,000, and 12.50 percent of librarians working in libraries serving areas with populations above 45,000.

The results were further broken out by the age of the librarians. By age, the group that finds Gmail to be the most useful are librarians under the age of 30; 100 percent of these librarians said Gmail is essential. The group that find Gmail to be the least useful are librarians aged 60-69; a 30 percent plurality of these librarians said Gmail is only somewhat useful while 20 percent do not use it. Librarians aged 70 or older are the only other group with at least some members who do not use Gmail, the 66.67 percent who do think the service is useful. A majority of librarians aged 30-39, 40-49, and 50-59 said Gmail is an essential feature.

Usefulness of Google Bookmarks

The public librarians next shared their opinions on the usefulness of Google Bookmarks. Of the entire sample, a majority 56.67 percent said they do not use Google Bookmarks, 16.67 percent said they are somewhat useful, 8.33 percent said they are useful, 3.33 percent said they are quite useful, and 11.67 percent said Google Bookmarks are essential. The remaining 3.33 percent did not answer the question.

The results were broken out by the libraries' annual budgets. Only 6.67 percent of librarians working in libraries with budgets below $50,000 per year said they use Google Bookmarks and all of them said they find the feature to be only somewhat useful. A plurality, 28.57 percent of the 50 percent of librarians working in libraries with annual budgets above $1,500,000 who do use Google Bookmarks also said they find the feature to be somewhat useful. In contrast, a 26.67 percent plurality of the 53.33 percent of librarians working in libraries with annual budgets between $300,000 and $1,500,000 who use Google Bookmarks said they find the feature to be essential. Fifty percent of librarians working in libraries with annual budgets between $50,000 and $300,000 use Google Bookmarks, 18.75 percent think Google Bookmarks is somewhat useful while an equal percent think the feature is essential. The remaining librarians were evenly split between useful and quite useful.

Usefulness of Google Patent Search

Next we asked the survey participants to share their thoughts on the usefulness of Google Patent Search. Very few of the participants use this Google feature, 80 percent said they do not. Of the entire sample, 8.33 percent said when they do use Google Patent Search it is somewhat useful, 6.67 percent said it is useful, and 3.33 percent said Google Patent Search is quite useful. The remaining 1.67 percent did not answer the question.

The results were broken out by the population size of the libraries' service areas. None of the librarians employed in libraries with service area populations below 2,000 use Google Patent Search. 13.33 percent of librarians employed in libraries serving areas with populations between 2,000 and 10,000 said Google Patent Search is somewhat useful and another 13.33 percent said it is useful; the remainder do not use it. Of the 20 percent of librarians working in libraries serving areas with populations in the 10,000-45,000 range, 6.67 percent used each of the following phrases to describe Google Patent Search's usefulness to them: somewhat useful, useful, and quite useful. Of the librarians working in libraries with service area populations larger than 45,000, 12.50 percent find Google Patent Search to be somewhat useful, 6.25 percent say it is useful, and another 6.25 percent find the feature quite useful.

The results were further broken out by the librarians' ages. Librarians under the age of 30 and librarians aged 70 or older in the sample do not use Google Patent Search. Librarians aged 30-39 use Google Patent Search most often and find it to be the most useful, 14.29 percent said it is useful while 28.57 percent said it is quite useful, they were the only group to describe it as such. Next, 25 percent of librarians aged 40-49 said they find Google Patent Search to be useful while the other 16.67 percent who use the feature said they find it to be just somewhat useful. The 8 percent of librarians aged 50-59 and 10 percent of librarians aged 60-69 who use Google Patent Search say the feature is just somewhat useful to them.

Usefulness of Google Forms

We asked the survey participants, "When you use Google Forms, how useful is it to you?" Of the entire sample, 58.33 percent said they do not use Google Forms, 6.67 percent said it is not very useful, 5 percent said it is somewhat useful, 13.33 percent said it is useful, 10 percent said it is quite useful, and 5 percent said it is essential. The remaining 1.67 percent did not comment on the usefulness of Google Forms.

The results were broken out by the libraries annual budgets. Librarians working in the lowest annual budget bracket were the only group to not have at least one member say that Google Forms is quite useful. 6.67 percent of librarians working in libraries with annual budgets under $50,000 and 13.33 percent of librarians working in libraries with annual budgets in the $300,000-$1,500,000 range said the feature is essential. 13.33 percent of librarians in the $300,000-$1,500,000 library annual budget bracket also said when they use Google Forms the feature isn't very useful at all. The only other group to say they do not find Google Forms to be very useful were librarians working in libraries with annual budgets between $50,000 and $300,000, 6.67 percent answered thus. A 21.43 percent plurality of librarians who use Google Forms and work in libraries with annual budgets above $1,500,000 said Google Forms is useful to them.

Usefulness of Google Slides

The public librarians then shared their opinions on the usefulness of Google Slides. Once more, most of the participants do not use this Google feature. Of the entire sample, 71.67 percent said they do not use Google Slides and 1.67 percent did not answer the question, 3.33 percent said they do use Google Slides but it is not very useful, 10 percent said it is somewhat useful, 6.67 percent said it is useful, 3.33 percent said it is quite useful, and 1.67 percent said it is essential.

The results were broken out by the libraries' service area populations. None of the librarians working in libraries with service area populations below 2,000 use Google Slides. The only librarian who uses Google Slides and finds the feature to be essential works in a library with a service area population greater than 45,000. 6.67 percent of librarians working in libraries serving area populations in the 10,000 to 45,000 range and 6.25 percent of those working in libraries with service area populations of more than 45,000 are also very positive about the usefulness of Google Slides; they said the feature is quite useful. The only group of librarians to say Google Slides is not very useful were those working in libraries with service area populations between 2,000 and 10,000. All of the other librarians who use Google Slides said it is either somewhat useful or useful.

The results were further broken out by the age of the librarians. The younger librarians surveyed find Google Slides to be the most useful. All 33.33 percent of librarians under the age of 30 who use Google Slides said it is essential to them. Of the librarians aged 30-39 who use the feature, 28.57 percent said it is quite useful and 28.57 percent said it is useful. In contrast, none of the librarians over the age of 70 use Google Slides and the 10 percent of those aged 60-69 who use the feature said it is just somewhat useful to them. In the middle of the age brackets, 8.33 percent of librarians aged 40-49 and 4 percent of those aged 50-59 said they find Google Slides to be not very useful at all but most of the librarians in these brackets who use the feature described it as being somewhat useful.

Usefulness of Google Groups

We asked the public librarians, "When you use Google Groups how useful is it to you?" Of the entire sample, 5 percent said Google Groups is not very useful, 13.33 percent said it is somewhat useful, 11.67 percent said it is useful, 3.33 percent said it is quite useful, and 1.67 percent said Google Groups is essential. 63.33 percent of the participants said they do not use Google Groups and the remaining 1.67 percent did not comment on the usefulness of this Google feature.

The results were broken out by the population size of the areas served by the libraries. Most of the librarians who use Google Groups said they find the feature to be somewhat useful or useful. Two groups of librarians who use Google Groups find the feature to be not very useful at all: 13.33 percent of librarians working in libraries serving area populations of 2,000-10,000 and 6.67 percent of librarians working in libraries serving area populations of 10,000-45,000. Two groups of librarians also find Google Groups to be quite useful: once more, 6.67 percent of librarians working in the 10,000-45,000 area population bracket and 6.25 percent of those working in libraries with service area populations greater than 45,000. The only librarian to say they use Google Groups and find the feature to be essential was one employed in a library with a service area population in the 2,000-10,000 range.

The results were further broken out by gender. Overall, male librarians find Google Groups to be more useful than female librarians do; they also use it more often. A 40 percent plurality of male librarians who use Google Groups find the feature to be quite useful. The remaining 20 percent of male librarians who use Google Groups said it is useful to them. None of the female librarians who use Google Groups said it is quite useful, but one did say they find the feature to be essential. Of the 32.73 percent of female librarians who do use Google Groups, a 14.55 percent plurality said it is somewhat useful and 5.45 percent said it is not very useful.

Usefulness of Google Analytics

The survey participants gave their opinions on the usefulness of Google Analytics. While a majority of the participants do not use Google Analytics, those who do tend to be positive about the usefulness of the feature. Of the entire sample, just 3.33 percent said they find Google Analytics to not be very useful, 10 percent said it is somewhat useful, 8.33 percent said it is useful, 8.33 percent said it is quite useful, and another 8.33 percent said it is essential. The remaining 61.67 percent of the public librarians surveyed do not use Google Analytics.

The results were broken out by the libraries' annual budgets. Librarians working in libraries with annual budgets between $50,000 and $300,000 were the only group with no member who does not find Google Analytics to be very useful at all. The percentages of librarians who only consider Google Analytics to be somewhat useful are: 12.50 percent of librarians working in libraries with budgets between $50,000 and $30,000 per year, 20 percent of those in the $300,000-$1,500,000 budget bracket, and 7.14 percent of those working in libraries with annual budgets above $1,500,000. In contrast, 6.25 percent of librarians working in the $50,000-$300,000 budget bracket, 6.67 percent of those in the $300,000-$1,500,000 budget bracket, and a plurality 21.43 percent of those working in libraries with annual budgets above $1,500,000 said they find Google Analytics to be essential. All of the librarians who use Google Analytics and work in libraries with annual budgets below $50,000 said the feature was either useful or quite useful.

The results were further broken out by the librarians' ages. None of the librarians under the age of 30 or those over 70 use Google Analytics. Of those who do use Google Analytics, librarians aged 60-69 are least impressed with the features usefulness. Of the 30 percent of librarians aged 60-69 who use Google Analytics, 10 percent said it is not very useful and 20 percent said it is only somewhat useful. Librarians aged 30-39 find Google Analytics to be the most useful; all of these librarians who use this feature rated it either quite useful or essential, 28.57 percent each. Librarians aged 40-49 are the most likely to use Google

Analytics, 75 percent do. Of the librarians in the 40-49 year age range, 25 percent think Google Analytics is essential, 25 percent think it is useful, 16.67 percent think it is quite useful, and 8.33 percent think it is just somewhat useful. A 12 percent plurality of librarians aged 50-59 who use Google Analytics said they find the feature to be somewhat useful; they were the only other group to say it was not very useful, 4 percent did, and none consider the feature to be essential.

Usefulness of Blogger

We asked the survey participants, "When you use Blogger, how useful is it to you?" Of the entire sample, 6.67 percent said Blogger is not very useful, 6.67 percent said it is somewhat useful, 5 percent said it is useful, 3.33 percent said it is quite useful and 5 percent said it is essential. A 71.67 percent majority of the public librarians in the sample said they do not use Blogger and 1.67 percent did not answer the question.

The results were broken out by the population size of the areas served by the libraries. Those with very positive opinions of the usefulness of Blogger are librarians working in libraries with service area populations greater than 45,000, librarians working in libraries with service area populations of 10,000-45,000 and librarians working in libraries with service area populations of 2,000-10,000; one librarian from all of these groups said Blogger is essential to them. 6.67 percent of librarians working in libraries with service area populations between 2,000 and 10,000 and 7.14 percent of librarians working in libraries with less than 2,000 rated Blogger "quite useful." At the other end of the spectrum librarians from libraries in the middle two population brackets both said Blogger is not very useful. A 25 percent plurality of librarians employed in libraries with the largest service area populations said Blogger is just somewhat useful; they were the only group to use this term to describe Blogger's usefulness.

The results were further broken out by the librarians' gender. Female librarians find Blogger to be much more useful than male librarians do. Of the male librarians surveyed, 80 percent do not use Blogger and the 20 percent who do use the feature said it is not very useful. More than three quarters of the female librarians surveyed use Blogger; 5.45 percent said it is not very useful, 7.27 percent said it is somewhat useful, 5.45 percent said it is useful, 3.64 percent said it is quite useful, and 5.45 percent said it is essential.

Usefulness of YouTube

The survey participants shared their opinions on the usefulness of YouTube. Of the entire sample, a 25 percent plurality said when they use YouTube it is useful, 21.67 percent said it is somewhat useful and another 21.67 percent said it is essential, 18.33 percent said it is quite useful, and 6.67 percent said YouTube is not very useful. Just 5 percent of the public librarians surveyed said they do not use YouTube and 1.67 percent did not comment on the feature's usefulness.

The results were broken out by the ages of the participants. All of the librarians in the sample under the age of 30 use YouTube and all of them said the feature is essential. All of the librarians aged 70 or older also use YouTube but none of the described YouTube as being essential or even quite useful; they were equally divided between "not very useful," "somewhat useful," and "useful" in their estimations of YouTube's usefulness. Pluralities of librarians aged 40-49 and 50-59 both said when they use YouTube it is useful while a plurality of librarians aged 60-69 said it is just somewhat useful. Finally, a majority of librarians aged 30-39 were evenly split in their opinions of YouTube's usefulness; 28.57 percent said YouTube is essential while another 28.57 percent said it is just somewhat useful.

Quite Useful or Essential Google Features

Next we asked the survey participants, "For those Google features that you labelled "Quite Useful" or "Essential" what were these features and what do you use them for?" We received 45 responses to this open-ended question. The public librarians use Google's apps and features both professionally and in their personal lives. According to the survey participants, the most useful Google features help the librarians with communication, web browsing, design, organization, research, reference and "getting around." The public librarians identified more than 20 Google apps and features they feel are quite useful or essential.

The most frequently named Google features were: Gmail, Chrome, and Maps. At least ten librarians commented on the usefulness of each of these features. Gmail is the email of choice for many of the librarians sampled. One participant noted that Gmail is clean and simple. Chrome is the default web browser for a large number of the survey participants; it is helpful, fast, and can show multiple websites. The public librarians use Maps as their personal GPS, to get directions and locate places.

Some of the other more frequently named essential apps and features are: Drive, Calendar, Images, YouTube, Bookmarks, Advanced Search, and Translate. Three or more librarians commented on the usefulness of the above features, noting their helpfulness in information gathering, organization, communication, marketing etc. A few of the other apps and features named by the librarians were: Notifications, Books, Photos, Scholar, Earth, Docs, Groups, and Blogger.

Time Spent Using Google Maps

"Approximately how much time in the past month have you personally spent (in hours or fractions thereof) using Google Maps in connection with your work?" was the next question we asked the survey participants. Of the entire sample, the mean was 4.63 hours and the median was 1 hour. The public librarians spent a minimum 0 hour and maximum 100 hours using Google Maps in connection with their work in the past month.

The results were broken out by the population size of the areas served by the libraries. Librarians working in libraries serving area populations of 10,000-45,000 spent the most time on Google Maps in connection to their work in the past month, a mean 9.35 hours in a range of 0 to 100. Librarians working in libraries with service area populations of less than 2,000 spent the least amount of time on Google Maps, a mean 1.13 hours in a range of 0 to 5 hours. In the middle of the group, librarians working in libraries serving areas with populations of 2,000-10,000 spent a mean 4.09 hours using Google Maps in connection with their work and librarians working in libraries with service area populations above 45,000 spent a mean 3.62 hours on Google Maps last month.

Time Spent Using Google Advanced Search

We then asked the survey participants how much time they had personally spent in the last month using Google Advanced Search in connection with their work. Of the entire sample, the mean was 4.58 hours and the median was 0 hours in a range of 0 to 100 hours.

The results were broken out by the libraries' annual budget figures. Librarians employed in libraries with annual budgets in the range of $300,000 to $1,500,000 spent the most time using Google Advanced Search in connection with their work in the past month: a mean 8.84 hours and median 1 hour in a range of 0 to 100 hours. At the other end of the spectrum, participants from libraries with budgets above $1,500,000 per year personally spent a mean 2.55 hours and 0 median hours, in a range of 0 to 12 hours, using Google Advanced Search in connection with their work. Librarians employed in institutions with an annual budget below $50,000 and those employed in libraries with budgets between $50,000 and $300,000 personally spent a mean 3.64 and 2.71 hours, respectively, using Google Advanced Search for work related purposes.

The results were further broken out by gender. Female librarians spent considerably more time using Google Advanced Search in connection to their work in the past month than male librarians did. Female librarians reported spending a mean 5.03 hours in a range of 0 to 100 hours using Google Advanced Search for work related purposes while male librarians reported spending only .08 hours mean, in a range of 0 to 2 hours. Male librarians did spend a median 1 hour using Advanced Search in the past month while the median figure for females was 0.

Time Spent Using Google Alerts

We asked the survey participants how much time they had personally spent using Google Alerts in the past month, in connection with their work. Of the entire sample, the mean was 2.43 hours and the median was 0 hours. Once more the librarians reported a range of 0 to 100 hours.

The results were broken out by the population size of the areas served by the libraries. Librarians employed in libraries serving area populations of 10,000-45,000 spent vastly more time using Google Alerts for work related purposes than the librarians in all the other area population brackets; they personally spent a mean 8.0 hours using the feature in the past month. The mean amounts of time the other librarians personally spent using Google Alerts for work in the past month were: 0.02 hours for librarians in libraries with service area populations below 2,000, 0.13 hours for those working in libraries with service area populations above 45,000, and 0.55 hours for those working in libraries serving areas with populations between 2,000 and 10,000.

Time Spent Using Google Notifications

We asked, "Approximately how much time in the past month have you personally spent (in hours or fractions thereof) using Google Notification in connection with your work?" Of the entire sample, the mean was 2.41 hours and the median was 0 hours. Again, the librarians reported spending a range of 0 to 100 hours using Google Notifications in connection with their work.

The results were again broken out by the population size of the areas served by the libraries. The librarians employed in libraries serving areas with populations greater than 45,000 reported spending no time at all in the past month using Google Notifications in connection with their work. In contrast, librarians employed in libraries serving areas with populations in the 10,000 to 45,000 range reported personally spending a mean 8.02 hours in a range of 0 to 100 hours using Google Notifications in connection with their work in the past month. In the middle, librarians in libraries with service area populations of less than 2,000 said they personally spent a mean 0.48 hours in a range of 0 to 5 hours in the past month using Google Notifications for work related purposes while librarians employed in libraries with service area populations in the range of 2,000 to 10,000 said they spent a mean 0.15 hours in a range of 0 to 1 hour using the feature.

Time Spent Using Google Images

The public librarians next shared the approximate amount of time they had personally spent using Google Images in connection with their work in the past month. Of the entire sample, the mean was 6.21 hours and the median was 1 hour in a range of 0 to 100 hours.

The results were broken out by the population size of the areas served by the libraries. Once more, librarians employed in libraries serving areas with populations in the range of 10,000-45,000 had spent the most time using the named Google feature. These librarians personally spent a mean 11.62 hours and median 2 hours using Google Images for work related purposes in the past month. Librarians from libraries with service area populations of more than 45,000 spent the least amount of time using Google Images for work, a mean 2.46 hours and median 1 hour in the past month. For librarians in libraries with service area populations below 2,000 the mean amount of time was 4.04 hours and for those in libraries with service area populations in the range of 2,000-10,000 the median was 6.64 hours.

The results were further broken out by age of librarian. Librarians aged 50-59 spent the highest mean amount of time using Google Images in connection with their work in the past month, 9.62 hours in a range of 0 to 100 hours. Librarians aged 30-39 spent a mean 7.67 hours in a range of just 0 to 25 hours using Google Images but their median figure was the highest overall at 5 hours. Librarians aged 70 or older spent the least amount of time using Google Images in connection with their work, just 0.17 hours mean in a range of 0 to .5 hours in the past month. Of the other age groups, librarians under the age of 30 personally spent a mean 2.33 hours using Google Images for work related purposes in the past month, those aged 40-49 spent a mean 3.21 hours, and those aged 60-69 spent a mean 2.94 hours using Google Images in connection with their work.

Time Spent Using Google Calendar

The public librarians then shared how much time they had spent in the past month using Google Calendar in connection with their work. Of the entire sample, the mean was 6.82 hours and the median was 0.50 hours in a range of 0 to 100 hours.

The results were broken out by the population size of the areas served by the libraries. Librarians in both the 2,000-10,000 and 10,000-45,000 area population brackets reported spending a range of 0 to 100 hours using Google Calendar in the past month. These librarians spent a mean 12.36 hours and a mean 10.69 hours, respectively, using Google Calendar for work related purposes. Librarians working in libraries serving area populations above 45,000 spent a mean 3.19 hours in a range of 0 to 25 hours using Google Calendar in connection with their work while librarians working in libraries serving area populations below 2,000 spent a mean 1.48 hours in a range of 0 to 8 hours using Google Calendar for work related purposes in the past month.

The results were further broken out by age of librarian. In the past month, the mean number of hours the librarians spent using Google Calendar in connection with their work were: 19.92 hours for librarians aged 40-49, 9.50 hours for librarians aged 30-39, 6.10 hours for librarians aged 50-59, 0.86 hours for librarians aged 60-69, 0.42 hours for librarians under the age of 30, and 0.25 hours for librarians aged 70 or older. Librarians in the 30-39 year age range were the only group to not report spending a minimum 0 hours using Google Calendar; these librarians spent a minimum 1 hour using Google Calendar in connection with their work in the past month.

Time Spent Using Google Chrome

We asked the survey participants how much time, in the past month, had they personally spent using Google Chrome in connection with their work. Of the entire sample, the mean was 33.88 hours and the median was 10 hours in a range of 0 to 160 hours.

The greatest range of results is seen when broken out by the age of the librarians. Librarians aged 30-39 personally spent the most time using Google Chrome for work related purposes in the past month; they spent a mean 68 hours and median 47 hours using the browser. These librarians reported spending a minimum 1 hour and maximum 160 hours using Chrome for work while librarians under the age of 30 reported spending a minimum of 6 hours and maximum 130 hours using the browser. Librarians under the age of 30 spent a mean 58.67 hours and median 40 hours using Chrome for work related purposes in the past month. Next, librarians in the 40-49 age range spent a mean 48.32 hours in a range of 0.25 to 120 hours using Google Chrome in connection with their work. Librarians aged 50-59 followed, having spent a mean 27.52 hours in a range of 0 to 125 hours in the past month using Google Chrome for work related purposes. Librarians in the 60-69 age range reported spending the second smallest amount of time using Google Chrome in connection with work: a mean 15.22 hours in a range of 0-120 hours. Finally, librarians aged 70 or older spent the least amount of time using Google Chrome in connection with their work in the past month: a mean 6.67 hours in a range of just 0 to 20 hours. Librarians aged 70 or older were the only group who spent a median 0 hours using Google Chrome for work related purposes in the past month.

The results were further broken out by gender. Female librarians reported spending a higher maximum number of hours using Google Chrome for work related purposes than did male librarians, 160 hours vs.140 hours. Male librarians, on the other hand, spent more time overall using the Google browser. Male librarians said they spent a mean 44.40 hours and median 12 hours using Google Chrome for work related purposes in the past month while female librarians personally spent a mean 32.62 hours and median 10 hours using Chrome in connection with their work.

Time Spent Using Google Books

"Approximately how much time in the past month have you personally spent using Google Books in connection with your work?" was the next question we asked the public librarians. Of the entire sample, the mean was just 0.81 hours and the median was 0 hours in a range of 0 to 10 hours.

The results were broken out by the libraries' annual budgets. Both librarians working in libraries with annual budgets in the $50,000- $300,000 range and librarians working in libraries with annual budgets in the $300,000-$1,500,000 range spent a mean 0.5 hours using Google Books in connection with their work in the past month, but librarians in the former group spent a maximum of just 2 hours while librarians in the latter group spent a maximum of 5 hours. Librarians employed in libraries with annual budgets below $50,000 spent the least amount of time using Google Books in connection with their work, a mean 0.18 hours in a range of 0 to 2 hours. Librarians working in libraries with annual budgets of more than $1,500,000 spent the most time using Google Books in connection with their work, a mean 2.26 hours in a range of 0 to 10 hours.

The results were further broken out by whether the librarians were male or female. Female librarians spent more time than male librarians using Google Books. In the past month, the female librarians surveyed said they personally spent a mean 0.86 hours, in a range of 0 to 10 hours, using Google Books in connection with their work. In contrast, the male librarians said they personally spent a mean 0.40 hours, in a range of 0 to 2 hours, using the feature for work related purposes.

Time Spent Using Google Scholar

The public librarians then shared how much time they personally spent in a month using Google Scholar in connection with their work. Of the entire sample, the librarians spend a mean 0.46 hours and median 0 hours, with a maximum of 10 hours, using Google Scholar for work related purposes.

The results were broken out by the population size of the areas served by the libraries. Librarians working in libraries serving areas with populations below 2,000 said they did not spend any time using Google Scholar in connection with their work in the past month. In contrast, librarians working in libraries with service area populations above 45,000 spent a mean 1.08 hours, in a range of 0 to ten hours, using Google Scholar for work related purposes in the past month. In the middle of the group, librarians in the 2,000 to 10,000 area population bracket spent a mean 0.10 hours, in a range of 0 to 1 hours, using Google Scholar and those in the 10,000 to 45,000 area population bracket spent a mean 0.54 hours, in a range of 0 to 2 hours, using Google in connection with their work in the past month.

Time Spent Using Google Translate

We then asked the librarians: Approximately how much time in the past month have you personally spent using Google Translate in connection with your work? Of the entire sample, the mean was 0.74 hours and the median was 0 hours. The survey participants spent a maximum 10 hours using Google Translate for work related purposes in the past month.

The results were again broken out by the population size of the areas served by the libraries. Librarians employed in libraries with the smallest service area populations spent the least amount of time using Google Translate in connection with their work: a mean 0.02 hours, in a range of 0 to 0.20 hours. Librarians employed in libraries serving area populations of 2,000-10,000 spent slightly more time, a mean 0.38 hours with a maximum 2 hours. In contrast, librarians working in libraries with a service area population of 10,000-45,000 spent a mean 1.23 hours and median 1 hour, in a range of 0 to 5 hours, using Google Translate in connection with their work in the past month. Librarians working in libraries serving area populations greater than 45,000 reported the largest range, 0 to 10 hours, but their mean and median times spent using Google Translate for work were 1.17 hours and 0.25 hours, respectively.

The greatest variance in results is seen when broken out by the age of the participants. The group that uses Google Translate the least are librarians aged 70 or older. In the past month these librarians did not spend any time using Google Translate in connection with their work. In contrast, librarians aged 40-49 spent a mean 2 hours and median 0.5 hours, in a range of 0 to 10 hours, using Google Translate for work related purposes in the past month. Librarians under the age of 30 had the highest median figure, 1 hour, but they spent a mean 0.67 hours, in a range of 0 to 1 hours, using Google Translate for work related purposes in the past month. Of the remaining groups, librarians aged 30-39 spent a mean .0.83 hours with a maximum 3 hours using Google Translate, those aged 60-69 spent a mean 0.69 hours with a maximum 1hour using the feature, and librarians aged 50-59 spent just 0.39 hours mean with a maximum of 5 hours using Google Translate in connection with their work in the past month.

Time Spent Using Google Public Data Explorer

The survey participants shared how much time they had personally spent using Google Public Data Explorer in connection with their work in the past month. The librarians spent very little time using Public Data Explorer. Of the entire sample, the mean was just 0.04 hours and the median was 0 in a range of 0 to 2 hours. Only one participant said they spent any time using Google Public Data Explorer for work related purposes in the past month: a female librarian in the 50-59 year age range, working in a library with a service area population between 10,000 and 45,000 and an annual budget in the $300,000 to $1,500,000 range.

Time Spent Using Google Drive

The public librarians then shared how much time they had personally spent using Google Drive in connection with their work in the past month. Of the entire sample, the mean was 5.57 hours and the median was 0 hours. The librarians spent a maximum 100 hours using Google Drive for work related purposes in the past month.

The results were broken out by the libraries' annual budgets. The librarians employed in libraries with annual budgets between $300,000 and $1,500,000 spent the most time using Google Drive in connection with their work in the past month: a mean 13.64 hours in a range of 0 to 100 hours. Librarians employed in libraries with budgets in the range of $50,000-$300,000 per year spent the least amount of time using Google Drive in connection with work: a mean 1.17 hours in a range of 0 to 10 hours. In the middle of the group, librarians working in libraries with annual budgets below $50,000 spent a mean 4.18 hours using Google Drive in connection with their work in the past month and librarians working in libraries with annual budgets above $1,500,000 spent a mean 2.23 hours using the feature.

The greatest range of results is seen when the results are broken out by the age of the librarians. Librarians aged 70 or older did not spend any time using Google Drive in connection with their work in the past month. Librarians aged 30-39 spent the most time using Google Drive for work related purposes in the past month: a mean 12.5 hours and median 10 hours in a range of 0 to 25 hours. Next, librarians aged 40-49 spent a mean 7.21 hours and median 3 hours using Google Drive. Librarians aged 50-59 reported a maximum of 100 hours spent using Google Drive in connection with work, but their mean was just 6.65 hours and their median was 0 hours. Librarians under the age of 30 spent a mean 2.33 hours and median 2 hours using Google Drive for work in the past month and librarians aged 60-69 spent a mean 0.33 hours and median 0 hours using the Google feature.

Time Spent Using Google Earth

We asked the survey participants, "Approximately how much in the past months have you personally spent using Google Earth in connection with your work?" Of the entire sample, the mean was 0.59 hours and the median was 0 hours, in a range of 0 to 5 hours.

The results were broken out by the libraries' annual budgets. Librarians working in libraries with budgets between $50,000 and $300,000 per year spent the most time using Google Earth in connection with their work in the past month while librarians working in libraries with budgets between $300,000 and $1,500,000 spent the least: means of 1 hour and 0.27 hours, respectively. In the middle of the group, librarians working in libraries with annual budgets above $1,500,000 spent a mean 0.73 hours using Google Earth for work related purposes and librarians working in libraries with annual budgets below $50,000 spent a mean 0.36 hours using the feature for work related purposes in the past month.

Time Spent Using Google Sky

The survey participants shared how much time they had personally spent in the past month using Google Sky in connection with their work. The public librarians spent very little time using the feature. Of the entire sample, the mean was 0.01 hours and the median was 0 hours, in a range of 0 to 0.5 hours. Again, just one librarian claimed to have spent time using Google Sky for work related purposes in the past month: a 60 to 69 year old female librarian employed in a library with an annual budget above $1,500,000 and a service area population of more than 45,000.

Time Spent Using Google+

Next we asked the survey participants to share how much time they had personally spent in the past month using Google+ in connection with their work. Of the entire sample the mean was 1.13 hours and the median was 0 hours. The public librarians spent a minimum 0 hours and a maximum 30 hours using Google+ for work related purposes in the past month.

The results were broken out by the population size of the areas served by the libraries. Librarians employed in libraries serving areas with populations below 2,000 did not spend any time using Google+ in connection with their work in the past month. In contrast, librarians employed in libraries serving areas with populations above 45,000 spent the most time using the social networking platform: a mean 2.50 hours in a range of 0 to 30 hours. Of the middle two population brackets, librarians working in libraries serving populations in the 2,000-10,000 range spent a mean 0.64 hours using Google+ in connection with their work in the past month and librarians working in libraries serving populations in the 10,000- 45,000 range said they spent a mean 1.23 hours using the feature for work related purposes.

The results were further broken out by gender. In the past month, the male librarians we surveyed spent more time, on average, using Google+ in connection with their work than the female librarians did. Male librarians spent a mean 2 hours using Google+ for work related purposes while female librarians only spent a mean 1.02 hours using the social networking feature. The female librarians we surveyed did spend a maximum 30 hours using Google+ while the male librarians spent a maximum 10 hours using the feature for work in the past month.

Time Spent Using Google Hangouts

We asked the survey participants, "Approximately how much time in the past month have you personally spent using Google Hangouts in connection with your work?" Of the entire sample, the mean was 3.57 hours and the median was 0 hours. The librarians reported personally spending a minimum 0 hours and maximum 160 hours in the past month using Google Hangouts in connection with their work.

The results were broken out by the age of the survey participants. A 30-39 year old librarian spent the maximum 160 hours using Google Hangouts for work related purposes in the past month. The mean time spent using this feature for librarians in the 30 to 39 year age bracket was 27.17 hours and the median was 0.5 hours; they were the only group to not have 0 as their median figure. In contrast, neither librarians under the age of 30 nor those aged 70+ spent any time using Google Hangouts for work related purposes in the past month. The mean times for the remaining age groups were: 0.21 hours for those aged 40-49, 0.22 hours for those aged 60 to 69, and 0.25 hours for those aged 50 to 59.

Time Spent Using Gmail

Next we asked the public librarian to share how much time they had personally spent using Gmail in connection with their work in the past month. Of the entire sample, the mean was

30.27 hours and the median was 5.50 hours. The public librarians spent a minimum 0 hours and a maximum 200 hours using Gmail for work related purposes in the past month.

The greatest range of results is seen when broken out by age. In the past month, librarians under the age of 30 spent the most time using Gmail in connection with their work: a mean 90 hours and median 100 hours, in a range of 40 to 130 hours. Librarians aged 30-39 spent a maximum 160 hours using Gmail for work related purposes but their mean was just 36.66 hours and their median was 14 hours. Librarians aged 40-49 spent a maximum 200 hours in the past month using Gmail in connection with their work; their mean was 68.43 hours and their median was 14 hours. For librarians aged 50-59, the mean amount of time they spent using Gmail for work related purposes in the past month was 15.77hours and the median was 2.25 hours, in a range of 0 hours to 120 hours and for those aged 60 to 69 the mean was 18.17 hours and the median was 3 hours, in a range of 0 to120 hours. Finally, while the librarians aged 70 or older spent the least amount time using Gmail for work related purposes in the past month, all of them did use the feature, a mean 2.33 hours and median 2 hours with a maximum of just 4 hours. Librarians aged 70 or older spent a minimum 1 hour in the past month using Gmail for work related purposes.

The results were further broken out by the libraries' annual budgets. Librarians working in libraries with annual budgets in the $300,000- $1,500,000 range spent the most time in the past month using Gmail for work related purposes: a mean 54.38 hours and median 30 hours, in a range of 0 to 200 hours. In contrast, librarians working in libraries with budgets below $50,000 per year spent the least amount of time using Gmail for work related purpose: a mean 8.32 hours and median 3 hours, in a range of 0 to 30 hours. The mean amount of time the other two groups spent were 20.27 hours for those in the $50,000-$300,000 budget bracket and 35.55 hours for those with annual budgets above $1,500,000.

Time Spent Using Google Bookmarks

We asked the survey participants, "Approximately how much time in the past month have you personally spent using Google Bookmarks in connection with your work?" Of the entire sample, the mean was 0.99 hours and the median was 0 hours, in a range of 0 to 20 hours.

The results were broken out by the population size of the areas served by the libraries. Librarians working in libraries serving area populations of 10,000-45,000 spent the most time using Google Bookmarks in connection with their work in the past month: a mean 2.69 hours with a maximum of 20 hours. At the other end of the spectrum, librarians employed in libraries with service area populations above 45,000 spent the least amount of time using Google Bookmarks for work related purposes: a mean 0.08 hours with a maximum of 0.5 hours in the past month. Librarians employed in libraries with service area populations below 20,000 and between 20,000 and 10,000 spent a mean 0.64 and a mean 0.24 hours, respectively, using Google Bookmarks in connection with their work in the past month.

The results were further broken out by gender. In the past month, the male librarians we surveyed did not spend any time using Google Bookmarks for work related purposes. In contrast, female librarians personally spent a mean 1.11 hours in the past month using Google Bookmarks in connection with their work.

Time Spent Using Google Patent Search

We asked the survey participants to share how much time they had personally spent using Google Patent Search in connection with their work in the past month. None of the librarians surveyed had spent any time at all using Google Patent Search for work related purposes in the past month.

Time Spent Using Google Forms

We asked the public librarians, "Approximately how much time in the past month have you personally spent using Google Forms in connection with your work?" Of the entire sample, the mean was 0.50 hours and the median was 0 hours, in a range of 0 to 10 hours.

The greatest range of results is seen when broken out by the age of the librarians. None of the librarians aged 70 or older spent any time in the past month using Google Forms in connection with their work. In contrast, librarians aged 60-69 spent a mean 1.44 hours, in a range of 0 to 10 hours, using Google Forms for work related purposes in the past month. The mean amounts of time the other librarians personally spent using Google Forms in connection with their work in the past month were: 0.04 hours for those aged 50-59, 0.33 hours for those under the age of 30, 0.50 for those aged 30-39, and 0.86 hours for those aged 40-49.

Time Spent Using Google Slides

We asked the survey participants how much time they had personally spent using Google Slides in connection with work in the past month. The librarians spent very little time using this feature; of the entire sample, the mean was 0.07 hours and the median was 0 hours, in a range of 0 to 1 hours.

The results were broken out the libraries annual budgets. Three groups reported personally spending time using Google Slides for work related purposes in the past month. Librarians employed in libraries with annual budgets in the $300,000-$1,500,000 range spent a mean 0.02 hours using Google Slides in connection with their work in the past month, those employed in libraries with budgets in the $50,000-$300,000 range spent a mean 0.08 hours using the feature, and those employed in libraries with annual budgets above $1,500,000 spent a mean 0.20 hours using Google Slides for work related purposes in the past month.

Time Spent Using Google Groups

The public librarians surveyed shared the amount of time they had personally spent using Google Groups in connection with their work in the past month. Of the entire sample, the mean was 0.24 hours and the median was 0 hours, in a range of 0 to 10 hours.

The results were broken out by the population size of the areas served by the libraries. Librarians employed in libraries serving areas with population sizes in the 10,000-45,000 range did not spend any time in the past month using Google Groups in connection with their work. Librarians employed in libraries serving area populations between 2,000 and 10,000 spent a mean 1.02 hours in the past month using Google Groups for work related purposes. In the middle, librarians working in libraries with service area populations below 2,000 spent a mean 0.02 hours in the past month using Google Groups in connection with their work and librarians working in libraries with service area populations above 45,000 spent a mean 0.04 hours using the feature for work related purposes in the past month.

The results were further broken out by gender. Female librarians personally spent a mean 0.27 hours in the past month using Google Groups in connection with their work. Male librarians, on the other hand, did not use the feature for work related purposes at all in the past month.

Time Spent Using Google Analytics

The survey participants then shared how much time they had personally spent in the past month using Google Analytics in connection with their work. Of the entire sample the mean was 0.46 hours and the median was again 0 hours, in a range of 0 to 5 hours.

The results were broken out by the libraries' annual budgets. Librarians working in libraries with annual budgets below $50,000 spent the least amount of time using Google Analytics for work related purposes in the past month: a mean 0.09 hours with a maximum of 1 hour. Librarians working in libraries at the other end of the budget scale, with annual budgets above $1,500,000 spent the most time using the feature: a mean 1.10 hours with a maximum of 5 hours. In the middle, librarians working in libraries with annual budgets in the $50,000- $300,000 range spent a mean 0.17 hours using Google Analytics in the past month and librarians working in libraries with budgets in the $300,000- $1,500,000 range spent a mean 0.55 hours using the feature.

Time Spent Using Blogger

Next we asked the participants, "Approximately how much time in the past month have you personally spent using Blogger in connection with your work?" Of the entire sample, the mean was 1.35 hours and the median was 0 hours. The public librarians said they spent a minimum 0 hours and a maximum 50 hours using Blogger for work related purposes in the past month.

The results were broken out by the population size of the areas served by the libraries. Only two of the groups of librarians used Google Blogger in the past month in connection with their work: librarians working in libraries serving area populations of 2,000 to 10,000 and librarians working in libraries serving area populations of 10,000 to 45,000. The former group spent a mean 1.2 hours and a maximum 10 hours using Google Blogger in connection with their work while the latter spent a mean 3.85 hours and a maximum 50 hours using the feature for work purposes in the past month.

The results were further broken out by the participants' ages. Again, just two groups used Google Blogger in connection with their work in the past month. Librarians between the ages of 40 and 49 spent a mean 1.71 hours in the past month using Google Blogger for work related purposes. Librarians under the age of 30 spent a mean 16.67 hours using the feature in connection with their work.

Time Spent Using YouTube

We then asked the public librarians to share how much time they had personally spent using YouTube in the past month in connection with their work. Of the entire sample, the mean was 3.58 hours and the median was 1 hours. The librarians spent a minimum 0 hours and a maximum 30 hours using YouTube for work related purposes in the past month.

The results were broken out by the libraries' annual budgets. Librarians employed in libraries with annual budgets below $50,000 spent the most time using YouTube in connection with their work in the past month: a mean 8.23 hours and a median 4 hours, in a range of 0 to 30 hours. Librarians employed in libraries with annual budgets in the $50,000- $300,000 range followed; they spent a mean 3.19 hours and median 2 hours in the past month using YouTube in connection with their work. Librarians employed in libraries with annual budgets above $1,500,000 spent a mean 1.77 hours and median 1 hour using YouTube for work related purposes. Finally, librarians working in libraries with annual budgets in the range of $300,000-$1,500,000 spent the least amount of time using YouTube for work related purposes in the past month: a mean 1.41 hours and median 0.75 hours.

The results were further broken out by the age of the librarians. Librarians aged 70 or older used YouTube in connection with their work the least in the past month: a mean 0.17 hours, in a range of 0 to 0.5 hours. In contrast, librarians aged 30-39 spent a mean 6.50 hours with a maximum of 20 hours using YouTube for work related purposes in the past month. Librarians under the age of 30 were the only group to not report a minimum of 0 hours; these librarians spent a minimum 0.20 hours using YouTube in the past month but their mean time spent with the feature was just 0.73 hours. Librarians aged 50-59 spent a maximum 30 hours in the past month using YouTube for work related purposes; their mean time was 4.67 hours. The mean amount of time the other librarians spent using YouTube for work related purposes in the past month was: 1.43 hours for librarians aged 40-49 and 2.91 hours for librarians aged 60-69.

Other Useful Google Features

Our next question was "What other apps or features offered by Google but not listed above have your found useful and why?" Most of the public librarians did not have an answer for this open ended question. A few additional apps and features were identified by the librarians as being useful. Two participants said they find Google Shopper/Shopping to be useful as "sometime patrons want consumer advice help." One of the librarians stated that they appreciate the ability to sync information across devices while another said they like the ability to sync their work and personal calendars and view them in the same place.

Another participant said they like Google Reminders in conjunction with calendar as it helps alert them when they need to be at a meeting etc. News, Android, and Video search were other features the public librarians find to be useful.

Most Useful App or Feature

The survey participants then shared with us the single Google app or feature they felt has saved them the most time or made them much more productive. We received 45 responses to this open-ended question. Five participants said none of the Google apps or features have been particularly useful to them, have saved them time or made them more productive while one participant identified a non-Google based book borrowing website.

The four most popular features or apps, named by 6 to 8 participants each, are: Drive, Chrome, Images, and Gmail. Two participants gave reasons for these choices. Of Google Chrome, one participant said, "It's nice to have a reliable browser than can load all websites." A librarian from a library with a service area population between 10,000 and 45,000 said "Drive for sure. The ability to share files has become essential."

Other features that were identified multiple times as being particularly useful in helping the participants save time and be more productive are: Calendar, Maps, Search, and Advanced Search. Finally, one participant named each of the following features: Chat, Groups, Translate, and YouTube.

Apps or Features To Tell Your Peers About

To conclude our survey we asked the public librarians, "If there was one app or feature in Google that you would like to let your peers know about, which one would that be?" Twenty-eight participants identified Google apps or features they would tell their peers about. Again, Google Images, Chrome, Drive, Gmail and Maps were the most frequently cited apps or features. A number of participants also felt Google Books, Google Scholar, and Calendar are features worth telling their peers about. Other features or apps the public librarians would like to let their peers know about are: Docs, Translate, Hangouts, Groups, Advanced Search, and Google+.

Table 1.1 Your major personal role at the library would best be described as:

	reference or information literacy	research or subject specialist	administration	technical services or cataloging	special collections	acquisitions or collection development
Entire sample	8,33%	3,33%	80,00%	3,33%	1,67%	3,33%

Table 1.2 Your major personal role at the library would best be described as: Broken out by Population size of the area served

Population size of the area served	reference or information literacy	research or subject specialist	administration	technical services or cataloging	special collections	acquisitions or collection development
Less than 2000	0,00%	7,14%	92,86%	0,00%	0,00%	0,00%
2000 - 10000	0,00%	0,00%	93,33%	0,00%	0,00%	6,67%
10000+ - 45000	20,00%	0,00%	66,67%	13,33%	0,00%	0,00%
More than 45000	12,50%	6,25%	68,75%	0,00%	6,25%	6,25%

Table 1.3 Your major personal role at the library would best be described as: Broken out by Age range of survey participant

Age range of survey participant	reference or information literacy	research or subject specialist	administration	technical services or cataloging	special collections	acquisitions or collection development
Under 30	33,33%	33,33%	33,33%	0,00%	0,00%	0,00%
30-39	14,29%	0,00%	71,43%	14,29%	0,00%	0,00%
40-49	8,33%	8,33%	66,67%	8,33%	8,33%	0,00%
50-59	4,00%	0,00%	88,00%	0,00%	0,00%	8,00%
60-69	10,00%	0,00%	90,00%	0,00%	0,00%	0,00%
70 or Over	0,00%	0,00%	100,00%	0,00%	0,00%	0,00%

Table 1.4 Your major personal role at the library would best be described as: Broken out by Library's annual budget, $

Library's annual budget, $	reference or information literacy	research or subject specialist	administration	technical services or cataloging	special collections	acquisitions or collection development
Less than 50000	0,00%	6,67%	86,67%	0,00%	0,00%	6,67%
50000 - 300000	0,00%	0,00%	93,75%	6,25%	0,00%	0,00%
300000+ - 1500000	6,67%	0,00%	86,67%	0,00%	0,00%	6,67%
More than 1500000	28,57%	7,14%	50,00%	7,14%	7,14%	0,00%

Table 1.5 Your major personal role at the library would best be described as: Broken out by Gender of survey participant

Gender of survey participant	reference or information literacy	research or subject specialist	administration	technical services or cataloging	special collections	acquisitions or collection development
Male	40,00%	0,00%	40,00%	20,00%	0,00%	0,00%
Female	5,45%	3,64%	83,64%	1,82%	1,82%	3,64%

Table 2.1 What percentage of your total use of search engines would you estimate is accounted for by your use of the Google search engine?

	Mean	Median	Minimum	Maximum
Entire sample	81,12	90,00	5,00	100,00

Table 2.2 What percentage of your total use of search engines would you estimate is accounted for by your use of the Google search engine? Broken out by Population size of the area served

Population size of the area served	Mean	Median	Minimum	Maximum
Less than 2000	75,50	92,50	5,00	100,00
2000 - 10000	83,09	85,00	50,00	100,00
10000+ - 45000	80,17	92,50	30,00	100,00
More than 45000	85,70	90,00	50,00	99,00

Table 2.3 What percentage of your total use of search engines would you estimate is accounted for by your use of the Google search engine? Broken out by Age range of survey participant

Age range of survey participant	Mean	Median	Minimum	Maximum
Under 30	86,50	86,50	75,00	98,00
30-39	95,43	99,00	85,00	100,00
40-49	89,83	90,00	75,00	100,00
50-59	82,40	90,00	50,00	100,00
60-69	54,29	50,00	5,00	95,00
70 or Over	80,00	80,00	80,00	80,00

Table 2.4 What percentage of your total use of search engines would you estimate is accounted for by your use of the Google search engine? Broken out by Library's annual budget, $

Library's annual budget, $	Mean	Median	Minimum	Maximum
Less than 50000	78,75	90,00	5,00	100,00
50000 - 300000	70,00	75,00	30,00	100,00
300000+ - 1500000	88,85	98,00	30,00	100,00
More than 1500000	88,29	90,00	75,00	99,00

Table 2.5 What percentage of your total use of search engines would you estimate is accounted for by your use of the Google search engine? Broken out by Gender of survey participant

Gender of survey participant	Mean	Median	Minimum	Maximum
Male	87,40	99,00	50,00	99,00
Female	80,29	90,00	5,00	100,00

Table 3 How often do you use the following features of Google?

Table 3.1.1 How often do you use Google Maps?

	Never really use it	Seldom use it	Sometimes use it	Often Use it	Very often use it
Entire sample	3,33%	15,00%	21,67%	35,00%	25,00%

Table 3.1.2 How often do you use Google Maps? Broken out by Population size of the area served

Population size of the area served	Never really use it	Seldom use it	Sometimes use it	Often Use it	Very often use it
Less than 2000	0,00%	35,71%	14,29%	35,71%	14,29%
2000 - 10000	0,00%	13,33%	40,00%	26,67%	20,00%
10000+ - 45000	6,67%	13,33%	20,00%	33,33%	26,67%
More than 45000	6,25%	0,00%	12,50%	43,75%	37,50%

Table 3.1.3 How often do you use Google Maps? Broken out by Age range of survey participant

Age range of survey participant	Never really use it	Seldom use it	Sometimes use it	Often Use it	Very often use it
Under 30	0,00%	0,00%	0,00%	33,33%	66,67%
30-39	0,00%	14,29%	0,00%	57,14%	28,57%
40-49	0,00%	16,67%	33,33%	16,67%	33,33%
50-59	4,00%	12,00%	24,00%	44,00%	16,00%
60-69	10,00%	20,00%	20,00%	20,00%	30,00%
70 or Over	0,00%	33,33%	33,33%	33,33%	0,00%

Table 3.1.4 How often do you use Google Maps? Broken out by Library's annual budget, $

Library's annual budget, $	Never really use it	Seldom use it	Sometimes use it	Often Use it	Very often use it
Less than 50000	6,67%	20,00%	26,67%	33,33%	13,33%
50000 - 300000	6,25%	25,00%	25,00%	37,50%	6,25%
300000+ - 1500000	0,00%	6,67%	26,67%	26,67%	40,00%
More than 1500000	0,00%	7,14%	7,14%	42,86%	42,86%

Table 3.1.5 How often do you use Google Maps? Broken out by Gender of survey participant

Gender of survey participant	Never really use it	Seldom use it	Sometimes use it	Often Use it	Very often use it
Male	20,00%	0,00%	0,00%	60,00%	20,00%
Female	1,82%	16,36%	23,64%	32,73%	25,45%

Table 3.2.1 How often do you use Google Advanced Search?

	No Answer	Never really use it	Seldom use it	Sometimes use it	Often Use it	Very often use it
Entire sample	1,67%	10,00%	28,33%	26,67%	18,33%	15,00%

Table 3.2.2 How often do you use Google Advanced Search? Broken out by Population size of the area served

Population size of the area served	No Answer	Never really use it	Seldom use it	Sometimes use it	Often Use it	Very often use it
Less than 2000	0,00%	21,43%	42,86%	21,43%	7,14%	7,14%
2000 - 10000	0,00%	13,33%	20,00%	33,33%	33,33%	0,00%
10000+ - 45000	6,67%	6,67%	40,00%	26,67%	6,67%	13,33%
More than 45000	0,00%	0,00%	12,50%	25,00%	25,00%	37,50%

Table 3.2.3 How often do you use Google Advanced Search? Broken out by Age range of survey participant

Age range of survey participant	No Answer	Never really use it	Seldom use it	Sometimes use it	Often Use it	Very often use it
Under 30	0,00%	0,00%	0,00%	66,67%	33,33%	0,00%
30-39	0,00%	14,29%	14,29%	14,29%	28,57%	28,57%
40-49	0,00%	8,33%	33,33%	16,67%	33,33%	8,33%
50-59	0,00%	16,00%	32,00%	32,00%	8,00%	12,00%
60-69	10,00%	0,00%	30,00%	10,00%	20,00%	30,00%
70 or Over	0,00%	0,00%	33,33%	66,67%	0,00%	0,00%

Table 3.2.4 How often do you use Google Advanced Search? Broken out by Library's annual budget, $

Library's annual budget, $	No Answer	Never really use it	Seldom use it	Sometimes use it	Often Use it	Very often use it
Less than 50000	0,00%	6,67%	53,33%	20,00%	6,67%	13,33%
50000 - 300000	0,00%	18,75%	25,00%	37,50%	18,75%	0,00%
300000+ - 1500000	0,00%	6,67%	13,33%	33,33%	26,67%	20,00%
More than 1500000	7,14%	7,14%	21,43%	14,29%	21,43%	28,57%

Table 3.2.5 How often do you use Google Advanced Search? Broken out by Gender of survey participant

Gender of survey participant	No Answer	Never really use it	Seldom use it	Sometimes use it	Often Use it	Very often use it
Male	0,00%	0,00%	20,00%	40,00%	0,00%	40,00%
Female	1,82%	10,91%	29,09%	25,45%	20,00%	12,73%

Table 3.3.1 How often do you use Google Alerts?

	No Answer	Never really use it	Seldom use it	Sometimes use it	Often Use it	Very often use it
Entire sample	1,67%	55,00%	13,33%	18,33%	8,33%	3,33%

Table 3.3.2 How often do you use Google Alerts? Broken out by Population size of the area served

Population size of the area served	No Answer	Never really use it	Seldom use it	Sometimes use it	Often Use it	Very often use it
Less than 2000	0,00%	64,29%	14,29%	21,43%	0,00%	0,00%
2000 - 10000	0,00%	40,00%	13,33%	26,67%	13,33%	6,67%
10000+ - 45000	6,67%	60,00%	6,67%	20,00%	6,67%	0,00%
More than 45000	0,00%	56,25%	18,75%	6,25%	12,50%	6,25%

Table 3.3.3 How often do you use Google Alerts? Broken out by Age range of survey participant

Age range of survey participant	No Answer	Never really use it	Seldom use it	Sometimes use it	Often Use it	Very often use it
Under 30	0,00%	100,00%	0,00%	0,00%	0,00%	0,00%
30-39	0,00%	57,14%	0,00%	28,57%	14,29%	0,00%
40-49	0,00%	25,00%	16,67%	25,00%	25,00%	8,33%
50-59	4,00%	72,00%	8,00%	8,00%	4,00%	4,00%
60-69	0,00%	30,00%	30,00%	40,00%	0,00%	0,00%
70 or Over	0,00%	66,67%	33,33%	0,00%	0,00%	0,00%

Table 3.3.4 How often do you use Google Alerts? Broken out by Library's annual budget, $

Library's annual budget, $	No Answer	Never really use it	Seldom use it	Sometimes use it	Often Use it	Very often use it
Less than 50000	0,00%	66,67%	13,33%	20,00%	0,00%	0,00%
50000 - 300000	0,00%	62,50%	12,50%	18,75%	6,25%	0,00%
300000+ - 1500000	6,67%	46,67%	6,67%	13,33%	20,00%	6,67%
More than 1500000	0,00%	42,86%	21,43%	21,43%	7,14%	7,14%

Table 3.3.5 How often do you use Google Alerts? Broken out by Gender of survey participant

Gender of survey participant	No Answer	Never really use it	Seldom use it	Sometimes use it	Often Use it	Very often use it
Male	0,00%	80,00%	0,00%	0,00%	20,00%	0,00%
Female	1,82%	52,73%	14,55%	20,00%	7,27%	3,64%

Table 3.4.1 How often do you use Google Notifications?

	Never really use it	Seldom use it	Sometimes use it	Often Use it	Very often use it
Entire sample	51,67%	20,00%	18,33%	6,67%	3,33%

Table 3.4.2 How often do you use Google Notifications? Broken out by Population size of the area served

Population size of the area served	Never really use it	Seldom use it	Sometimes use it	Often Use it	Very often use it
Less than 2000	57,14%	28,57%	14,29%	0,00%	0,00%
2000 - 10000	33,33%	20,00%	26,67%	13,33%	6,67%
10000+ - 45000	66,67%	13,33%	13,33%	0,00%	6,67%
More than 45000	50,00%	18,75%	18,75%	12,50%	0,00%

Table 3.4.3 How often do you use Google Notifications? Broken out by Age range of survey participant

Age range of survey participant	Never really use it	Seldom use it	Sometimes use it	Often Use it	Very often use it
Under 30	66,67%	33,33%	0,00%	0,00%	0,00%
30-39	42,86%	0,00%	57,14%	0,00%	0,00%
40-49	33,33%	16,67%	25,00%	25,00%	0,00%
50-59	60,00%	24,00%	4,00%	4,00%	8,00%
60-69	50,00%	20,00%	30,00%	0,00%	0,00%
70 or Over	66,67%	33,33%	0,00%	0,00%	0,00%

Table 3.4.4 How often do you use Google Notifications? Broken out by Library's annual budget, $

Library's annual budget, $	Never really use it	Seldom use it	Sometimes use it	Often Use it	Very often use it
Less than 50000	73,33%	13,33%	13,33%	0,00%	0,00%
50000 - 300000	37,50%	31,25%	25,00%	6,25%	0,00%
300000+ - 1500000	53,33%	6,67%	20,00%	6,67%	13,33%
More than 1500000	42,86%	28,57%	14,29%	14,29%	0,00%

Table 3.4.5 How often do you use Google Notifications? Broken out by Gender of survey participant

Gender of survey participant	Never really use it	Seldom use it	Sometimes use it	Often Use it	Very often use it
Male	60,00%	0,00%	40,00%	0,00%	0,00%
Female	50,91%	21,82%	16,36%	7,27%	3,64%

Table 3.5.1 How often do you use Google Images?

	Never really use it	Seldom use it	Sometimes use it	Often Use it	Very often use it
Entire sample	8,33%	5,00%	28,33%	31,67%	26,67%

Table 3.5.2 How often do you use Google Images? Broken out by Population size of the area served

Population size of the area served	Never really use it	Seldom use it	Sometimes use it	Often Use it	Very often use it
Less than 2000	7,14%	0,00%	57,14%	14,29%	21,43%
2000 - 10000	13,33%	13,33%	13,33%	26,67%	33,33%
10000+ - 45000	13,33%	6,67%	26,67%	33,33%	20,00%
More than 45000	0,00%	0,00%	18,75%	50,00%	31,25%

Table 3.5.3 How often do you use Google Images? Broken out by Age range of survey participant

Age range of survey participant	Never really use it	Seldom use it	Sometimes use it	Often Use it	Very often use it
Under 30	0,00%	0,00%	0,00%	33,33%	66,67%
30-39	0,00%	0,00%	14,29%	28,57%	57,14%
40-49	8,33%	8,33%	8,33%	50,00%	25,00%
50-59	8,00%	4,00%	36,00%	28,00%	24,00%
60-69	10,00%	10,00%	40,00%	30,00%	10,00%
70 or Over	33,33%	0,00%	66,67%	0,00%	0,00%

Table 3.5.4 How often do you use Google Images? Broken out by Library's annual budget, $

Library's annual budget, $	Never really use it	Seldom use it	Sometimes use it	Often Use it	Very often use it
Less than 50000	20,00%	0,00%	33,33%	26,67%	20,00%
50000 - 300000	6,25%	12,50%	43,75%	6,25%	31,25%
300000+ - 1500000	6,67%	6,67%	20,00%	46,67%	20,00%
More than 1500000	0,00%	0,00%	14,29%	50,00%	35,71%

Table 3.5.5 How often do you use Google Images? Broken out by Gender of survey participant

Gender of survey participant	Never really use it	Seldom use it	Sometimes use it	Often Use it	Very often use it
Male	20,00%	0,00%	20,00%	40,00%	20,00%
Female	7,27%	5,45%	29,09%	30,91%	27,27%

Table 3.6.1 How often do you use Google Photos?

	No Answer	Never really use it	Seldom use it	Sometimes use it	Often Use it	Very often use it
Entire sample	3,33%	35,00%	11,67%	21,67%	20,00%	8,33%

Table 3.6.2 How often do you use Google Photos? Broken out by Population size of the area served

Population size of the area served	No Answer	Never really use it	Seldom use it	Sometimes use it	Often Use it	Very often use it
Less than 2000	0,00%	35,71%	7,14%	35,71%	14,29%	7,14%
2000 - 10000	0,00%	40,00%	6,67%	13,33%	26,67%	13,33%
10000+ - 45000	0,00%	33,33%	13,33%	26,67%	13,33%	13,33%
More than 45000	12,50%	31,25%	18,75%	12,50%	25,00%	0,00%

Table 3.6.3 How often do you use Google Photos? Broken out by Age range of survey participant

Age range of survey participant	No Answer	Never really use it	Seldom use it	Sometimes use it	Often Use it	Very often use it
Under 30	0,00%	33,33%	33,33%	0,00%	0,00%	33,33%
30-39	0,00%	14,29%	0,00%	28,57%	42,86%	14,29%
40-49	8,33%	33,33%	8,33%	25,00%	25,00%	0,00%
50-59	4,00%	44,00%	12,00%	16,00%	12,00%	12,00%
60-69	0,00%	30,00%	20,00%	20,00%	30,00%	0,00%
70 or Over	0,00%	33,33%	0,00%	66,67%	0,00%	0,00%

Table 3.6.4 How often do you use Google Photos? Broken out by Library's annual budget, $

Library's annual budget, $	No Answer	Never really use it	Seldom use it	Sometimes use it	Often Use it	Very often use it
Less than 50000	0,00%	26,67%	6,67%	33,33%	26,67%	6,67%
50000 - 300000	0,00%	43,75%	12,50%	25,00%	12,50%	6,25%
300000+ - 1500000	6,67%	40,00%	6,67%	6,67%	20,00%	20,00%
More than 1500000	7,14%	28,57%	21,43%	21,43%	21,43%	0,00%

Table 3.6.5 How often do you use Google Photos? Broken out by Gender of survey participant

Gender of survey participant	No Answer	Never really use it	Seldom use it	Sometimes use it	Often Use it	Very often use it
Male	0,00%	40,00%	0,00%	40,00%	20,00%	0,00%
Female	3,64%	34,55%	12,73%	20,00%	20,00%	9,09%

Table 3.7.1 How often do you use Google Calendar?

	Never really use it	Seldom use it	Sometimes use it	Often Use it	Very often use it
Entire sample	41,67%	8,33%	11,67%	6,67%	31,67%

Table 3.7.2 How often do you use Google Calendar? Broken out by Population size of the area served

Population size of the area served	Never really use it	Seldom use it	Sometimes use it	Often Use it	Very often use it
Less than 2000	42,86%	14,29%	7,14%	14,29%	21,43%
2000 - 10000	40,00%	6,67%	6,67%	13,33%	33,33%
10000+ - 45000	33,33%	6,67%	26,67%	0,00%	33,33%
More than 45000	50,00%	6,25%	6,25%	0,00%	37,50%

Table 3.7.3 How often do you use Google Calendar? Broken out by Age range of survey participant

Age range of survey participant	Never really use it	Seldom use it	Sometimes use it	Often Use it	Very often use it
Under 30	33,33%	0,00%	33,33%	0,00%	33,33%
30-39	0,00%	0,00%	0,00%	14,29%	85,71%
40-49	16,67%	16,67%	16,67%	8,33%	41,67%
50-59	56,00%	4,00%	8,00%	8,00%	24,00%
60-69	70,00%	10,00%	20,00%	0,00%	0,00%
70 or Over	33,33%	33,33%	0,00%	0,00%	33,33%

Table 3.7.4 How often do you use Google Calendar? Broken out by Library's annual budget, $

Library's annual budget, $	Never really use it	Seldom use it	Sometimes use it	Often Use it	Very often use it
Less than 50000	46,67%	13,33%	6,67%	13,33%	20,00%
50000 - 300000	50,00%	6,25%	18,75%	6,25%	18,75%
300000+ - 1500000	40,00%	0,00%	6,67%	6,67%	46,67%
More than 1500000	28,57%	14,29%	14,29%	0,00%	42,86%

Table 3.7.5 How often do you use Google Calendar? Broken out by Gender of survey participant

Gender of survey participant	Never really use it	Seldom use it	Sometimes use it	Often Use it	Very often use it
Male	40,00%	0,00%	0,00%	0,00%	60,00%
Female	41,82%	9,09%	12,73%	7,27%	29,09%

Table 3.8.1 How often do you use Chrome?

	Never really use it	Seldom use it	Sometimes use it	Often Use it	Very often use it
Entire sample	11,67%	8,33%	15,00%	18,33%	46,67%

Table 3.8.2 How often do you use Chrome? Broken out by Population size of the area served

Population size of the area served	Never really use it	Seldom use it	Sometimes use it	Often Use it	Very often use it
Less than 2000	28,57%	21,43%	14,29%	0,00%	35,71%
2000 - 10000	6,67%	6,67%	6,67%	40,00%	40,00%
10000+ - 45000	13,33%	6,67%	20,00%	26,67%	33,33%
More than 45000	0,00%	0,00%	18,75%	6,25%	75,00%

Table 3.8.3 How often do you use Chrome? Broken out by Age range of survey participant

Age range of survey participant	Never really use it	Seldom use it	Sometimes use it	Often Use it	Very often use it
Under 30	0,00%	0,00%	0,00%	0,00%	100,00%
30-39	0,00%	14,29%	0,00%	14,29%	71,43%
40-49	8,33%	16,67%	0,00%	33,33%	41,67%
50-59	8,00%	8,00%	12,00%	16,00%	56,00%
60-69	30,00%	0,00%	50,00%	10,00%	10,00%
70 or Over	33,33%	0,00%	33,33%	33,33%	0,00%

Table 3.8.4 How often do you use Chrome? Broken out by Library's annual budget, $

Library's annual budget, $	Never really use it	Seldom use it	Sometimes use it	Often Use it	Very often use it
Less than 50000	20,00%	20,00%	26,67%	13,33%	20,00%
50000 - 300000	18,75%	6,25%	12,50%	18,75%	43,75%
300000+ - 1500000	6,67%	0,00%	6,67%	33,33%	53,33%
More than 1500000	0,00%	7,14%	14,29%	7,14%	71,43%

Table 3.8.5 How often do you use Chrome? Broken out by Gender of survey participant

Gender of survey participant	Never really use it	Seldom use it	Sometimes use it	Often Use it	Very often use it
Male	20,00%	0,00%	0,00%	20,00%	60,00%
Female	10,91%	9,09%	16,36%	18,18%	45,45%

Table 3.9.1 How often do you use Google Books?

	Never really use it	Seldom use it	Sometimes use it	Often Use it	Very often use it
Entire sample	46,67%	21,67%	20,00%	3,33%	8,33%

Table 3.9.2 How often do you use Google Books? Broken out by Population size of the area served

Population size of the area served	Never really use it	Seldom use it	Sometimes use it	Often Use it	Very often use it
Less than 2000	78,57%	7,14%	7,14%	0,00%	7,14%
2000 - 10000	46,67%	26,67%	13,33%	6,67%	6,67%
10000+ - 45000	26,67%	40,00%	26,67%	6,67%	0,00%

More than 45000	37,50%	12,50%	31,25%	0,00%	18,75%

Table 3.9.3 How often do you use Google Books? Broken out by Age range of survey participant

Age range of survey participant	Never really use it	Seldom use it	Sometimes use it	Often Use it	Very often use it
Under 30	0,00%	0,00%	66,67%	0,00%	33,33%
30-39	14,29%	28,57%	14,29%	28,57%	14,29%
40-49	33,33%	25,00%	16,67%	0,00%	25,00%
50-59	60,00%	20,00%	20,00%	0,00%	0,00%
60-69	50,00%	30,00%	20,00%	0,00%	0,00%
70 or Over	100,00%	0,00%	0,00%	0,00%	0,00%

Table 3.9.4 How often do you use Google Books? Broken out by Library's annual budget, $

Library's annual budget, $	Never really use it	Seldom use it	Sometimes use it	Often Use it	Very often use it
Less than 50000	73,33%	6,67%	13,33%	0,00%	6,67%
50000 - 300000	43,75%	18,75%	18,75%	12,50%	6,25%
300000+ - 1500000	33,33%	40,00%	26,67%	0,00%	0,00%
More than 1500000	35,71%	21,43%	21,43%	0,00%	21,43%

Table 3.9.5 How often do you use Google Books? Broken out by Gender of survey participant

Gender of survey participant	Never really use it	Seldom use it	Sometimes use it	Often Use it	Very often use it
Male	40,00%	40,00%	0,00%	20,00%	0,00%
Female	47,27%	20,00%	21,82%	1,82%	9,09%

Table 3.10.1 How often do you use Google Scholar?

	Never really use it	Seldom use it	Sometimes use it	Often Use it	Very often use it
Entire sample	63,33%	16,67%	8,33%	6,67%	5,00%

Table 3.10.2 How often do you use Google Scholar? Broken out by Population size of the area served

Population size of the area served	Never really use it	Seldom use it	Sometimes use it	Often Use it	Very often use it
Less than 2000	92,86%	7,14%	0,00%	0,00%	0,00%
2000 - 10000	60,00%	26,67%	6,67%	0,00%	6,67%
10000+ - 45000	46,67%	20,00%	13,33%	20,00%	0,00%
More than 45000	56,25%	12,50%	12,50%	6,25%	12,50%

Table 3.10.3 How often do you use Google Scholar? Broken out by Age range of survey participant

Age range of survey participant	Never really use it	Seldom use it	Sometimes use it	Often Use it	Very often use it
Under 30	0,00%	33,33%	0,00%	33,33%	33,33%
30-39	42,86%	28,57%	0,00%	28,57%	0,00%
40-49	50,00%	16,67%	8,33%	8,33%	16,67%
50-59	76,00%	12,00%	12,00%	0,00%	0,00%
60-69	70,00%	20,00%	10,00%	0,00%	0,00%
70 or Over	100,00%	0,00%	0,00%	0,00%	0,00%

Table 3.10.4 How often do you use Google Scholar? Broken out by Library's annual budget, $

Library's annual budget, $	Never really use it	Seldom use it	Sometimes use it	Often Use it	Very often use it
Less than 50000	100,00%	0,00%	0,00%	0,00%	0,00%
50000 - 300000	50,00%	25,00%	12,50%	6,25%	6,25%
300000+ - 1500000	46,67%	26,67%	20,00%	6,67%	0,00%
More than 1500000	57,14%	14,29%	0,00%	14,29%	14,29%

Table 3.10.5 How often do you use Google Scholar? Broken out by Gender of survey participant

Gender of survey participant	Never really use it	Seldom use it	Sometimes use it	Often Use it	Very often use it
Male	40,00%	20,00%	0,00%	40,00%	0,00%
Female	65,45%	16,36%	9,09%	3,64%	5,45%

Table 3.11.1 How often do you use Google Scholar My Citations?

	Never really use it	Seldom use it	Sometimes use it	Often Use it	Very often use it
Entire sample	75,00%	15,00%	6,67%	1,67%	1,67%

Table 3.11.2 How often do you use Google Scholar My Citations? Broken out by Population size of the area served

Population size of the area served	Never really use it	Seldom use it	Sometimes use it	Often Use it	Very often use it
Less than 2000	100,00%	0,00%	0,00%	0,00%	0,00%
2000 - 10000	66,67%	20,00%	6,67%	0,00%	6,67%
10000+ - 45000	60,00%	20,00%	20,00%	0,00%	0,00%
More than 45000	75,00%	18,75%	0,00%	6,25%	0,00%

Table 3.11.3 How often do you use Google Scholar My Citations? Broken out by Age range of survey participant

Age range of survey participant	Never really use it	Seldom use it	Sometimes use it	Often Use it	Very often use it
Under 30	33,33%	66,67%	0,00%	0,00%	0,00%
30-39	71,43%	0,00%	28,57%	0,00%	0,00%
40-49	50,00%	25,00%	8,33%	8,33%	8,33%
50-59	88,00%	12,00%	0,00%	0,00%	0,00%
60-69	80,00%	10,00%	10,00%	0,00%	0,00%
70 or Over	100,00%	0,00%	0,00%	0,00%	0,00%

Table 3.11.4 How often do you use Google Scholar My Citations? Broken out by Library's annual budget, $

Library's annual budget, $	Never really use it	Seldom use it	Sometimes use it	Often Use it	Very often use it
Less than 50000	100,00%	0,00%	0,00%	0,00%	0,00%
50000 - 300000	68,75%	18,75%	6,25%	0,00%	6,25%
300000+ - 1500000	60,00%	26,67%	13,33%	0,00%	0,00%
More than 1500000	71,43%	14,29%	7,14%	7,14%	0,00%

Table 3.11.5 How often do you use Google Scholar My Citations? Broken out by Gender of survey participant

Gender of survey participant	Never really use it	Seldom use it	Sometimes use it	Often Use it	Very often use it
Male	60,00%	0,00%	40,00%	0,00%	0,00%
Female	76,36%	16,36%	3,64%	1,82%	1,82%

Table 3.12.1 How often do you use Google Translate?

	Never really use it	Seldom use it	Sometimes use it	Often Use it	Very often use it
Entire sample	33,33%	23,33%	30,00%	10,00%	3,33%

Table 3.12.2 How often do you use Google Translate? Broken out by Population size of the area served

Population size of the area served	Never really use it	Seldom use it	Sometimes use it	Often Use it	Very often use it
Less than 2000	42,86%	42,86%	14,29%	0,00%	0,00%
2000 - 10000	40,00%	13,33%	40,00%	0,00%	6,67%
10000+ - 45000	26,67%	33,33%	26,67%	13,33%	0,00%
More than 45000	25,00%	6,25%	37,50%	25,00%	6,25%

Table 3.12.3 How often do you use Google Translate? Broken out by Age range of survey participant

Age range of survey participant	Never really use it	Seldom use it	Sometimes use it	Often Use it	Very often use it
Under 30	33,33%	0,00%	0,00%	33,33%	33,33%
30-39	0,00%	28,57%	57,14%	14,29%	0,00%
40-49	41,67%	8,33%	25,00%	16,67%	8,33%
50-59	36,00%	24,00%	36,00%	4,00%	0,00%
60-69	40,00%	30,00%	20,00%	10,00%	0,00%
70 or Over	33,33%	66,67%	0,00%	0,00%	0,00%

Table 3.12.4 How often do you use Google Translate? Broken out by Library's annual budget, $

Library's annual budget, $	Never really use it	Seldom use it	Sometimes use it	Often Use it	Very often use it
Less than 50000	46,67%	46,67%	6,67%	0,00%	0,00%
50000 - 300000	43,75%	12,50%	31,25%	6,25%	6,25%
300000+ - 1500000	20,00%	20,00%	53,33%	6,67%	0,00%
More than 1500000	21,43%	14,29%	28,57%	28,57%	7,14%

Table 3.12.5 How often do you use Google Translate? Broken out by Gender of survey participant

Gender of survey participant	Never really use it	Seldom use it	Sometimes use it	Often Use it	Very often use it
Male	20,00%	0,00%	60,00%	20,00%	0,00%
Female	34,55%	25,45%	27,27%	9,09%	3,64%

Table 3.13.1 How often do you use Google Public Data Explorer?

	Never really use it	Seldom use it	Sometimes use it	Often Use it	Very often use it
Entire sample	75,00%	21,67%	3,33%	0,00%	0,00%

Table 3.13.2 How often do you use Google Public Data Explorer? Broken out by Population size of the area served

Population size of the area served	Never really use it	Seldom use it	Sometimes use it	Often Use it	Very often use it
Less than 2000	92,86%	7,14%	0,00%	0,00%	0,00%
2000 - 10000	60,00%	26,67%	13,33%	0,00%	0,00%
10000+ - 45000	80,00%	20,00%	0,00%	0,00%	0,00%
More than 45000	68,75%	31,25%	0,00%	0,00%	0,00%

Table 3.13.3 How often do you use Google Public Data Explorer? Broken out by Age range of survey participant

Age range of survey participant	Never really use it	Seldom use it	Sometimes use it	Often Use it	Very often use it
Under 30	100,00%	0,00%	0,00%	0,00%	0,00%
30-39	57,14%	42,86%	0,00%	0,00%	0,00%
40-49	58,33%	33,33%	8,33%	0,00%	0,00%
50-59	84,00%	16,00%	0,00%	0,00%	0,00%
60-69	70,00%	20,00%	10,00%	0,00%	0,00%
70 or Over	100,00%	0,00%	0,00%	0,00%	0,00%

Table 3.13.4 How often do you use Google Public Data Explorer? Broken out by Library's annual budget, $

Library's annual budget, $	Never really use it	Seldom use it	Sometimes use it	Often Use it	Very often use it
Less than 50000	93,33%	6,67%	0,00%	0,00%	0,00%
50000 - 300000	68,75%	18,75%	12,50%	0,00%	0,00%
300000+ - 1500000	73,33%	26,67%	0,00%	0,00%	0,00%
More than 1500000	64,29%	35,71%	0,00%	0,00%	0,00%

Table 3.13.5 How often do you use Google Public Data Explorer? Broken out by Gender of survey participant

Gender of survey participant	Never really use it	Seldom use it	Sometimes use it	Often Use it	Very often use it
Male	60,00%	40,00%	0,00%	0,00%	0,00%
Female	76,36%	20,00%	3,64%	0,00%	0,00%

Table 3.14.1 How often do you use Google Drive?

	Never really use it	Seldom use it	Sometimes use it	Often Use it	Very often use it
Entire sample	41,67%	11,67%	10,00%	6,67%	30,00%

Table 3.14.2 How often do you use Google Drive? Broken out by Population size of the area served

Population size of the area served	Never really use it	Seldom use it	Sometimes use it	Often Use it	Very often use it
Less than 2000	57,14%	7,14%	21,43%	0,00%	14,29%
2000 - 10000	40,00%	13,33%	13,33%	0,00%	33,33%
10000+ - 45000	40,00%	13,33%	0,00%	13,33%	33,33%
More than 45000	31,25%	12,50%	6,25%	12,50%	37,50%

Table 3.14.3 How often do you use Google Drive? Broken out by Age range of survey participant

Age range of survey participant	Never really use it	Seldom use it	Sometimes use it	Often Use it	Very often use it
Under 30	33,33%	0,00%	0,00%	0,00%	66,67%
30-39	0,00%	0,00%	14,29%	14,29%	71,43%
40-49	33,33%	8,33%	0,00%	8,33%	50,00%
50-59	44,00%	16,00%	16,00%	4,00%	20,00%
60-69	70,00%	10,00%	10,00%	10,00%	0,00%
70 or Over	66,67%	33,33%	0,00%	0,00%	0,00%

Table 3.14.4 How often do you use Google Drive? Broken out by Library's annual budget, $

Library's annual budget, $	Never really use it	Seldom use it	Sometimes use it	Often Use it	Very often use it
Less than 50000	60,00%	6,67%	13,33%	0,00%	20,00%
50000 - 300000	56,25%	18,75%	6,25%	0,00%	18,75%
300000+ - 1500000	20,00%	13,33%	13,33%	13,33%	40,00%
More than 1500000	28,57%	7,14%	7,14%	14,29%	42,86%

Table 3.14.5 How often do you use Google Drive? Broken out by Gender of survey participant

Gender of survey participant	Never really use it	Seldom use it	Sometimes use it	Often Use it	Very often use it
Male	40,00%	0,00%	0,00%	20,00%	40,00%
Female	41,82%	12,73%	10,91%	5,45%	29,09%

Table 3.15.1 How often do you use Gmail?

	Never really use it	Seldom use it	Sometimes use it	Often Use it	Very often use it
Entire sample	3,33%	10,00%	10,00%	16,67%	60,00%

Table 3.15.2 How often do you use Gmail? Broken out by Population size of the area served

Population size of the area served	Never really use it	Seldom use it	Sometimes use it	Often Use it	Very often use it
Less than 2000	0,00%	14,29%	14,29%	21,43%	50,00%
2000 - 10000	0,00%	6,67%	0,00%	13,33%	80,00%
10000+ - 45000	13,33%	6,67%	20,00%	13,33%	46,67%
More than 45000	0,00%	12,50%	6,25%	18,75%	62,50%

Table 3.15.3 How often do you use Gmail? Broken out by Age range of survey participant

Age range of survey participant	Never really use it	Seldom use it	Sometimes use it	Often Use it	Very often use it
Under 30	0,00%	0,00%	0,00%	0,00%	100,00%
30-39	0,00%	0,00%	14,29%	14,29%	71,43%
40-49	0,00%	25,00%	0,00%	8,33%	66,67%
50-59	0,00%	12,00%	4,00%	16,00%	68,00%
60-69	20,00%	0,00%	30,00%	30,00%	20,00%
70 or Over	0,00%	0,00%	33,33%	33,33%	33,33%

Table 3.15.4 How often do you use Gmail? Broken out by Library's annual budget, $

Library's annual budget, $	Never really use it	Seldom use it	Sometimes use it	Often Use it	Very often use it
Less than 50000	0,00%	6,67%	6,67%	40,00%	46,67%
50000 - 300000	6,25%	12,50%	12,50%	6,25%	62,50%
300000+ - 1500000	6,67%	6,67%	6,67%	13,33%	66,67%
More than 1500000	0,00%	14,29%	14,29%	7,14%	64,29%

Table 3.15.5 How often do you use Gmail? Broken out by Gender of survey participant

Gender of survey participant	Never really use it	Seldom use it	Sometimes use it	Often Use it	Very often use it
Male	20,00%	0,00%	20,00%	20,00%	40,00%
Female	1,82%	10,91%	9,09%	16,36%	61,82%

Table 3.16.1 How often do you use Google Earth?

	No Answer	Never really use it	Seldom use it	Sometimes use it	Often Use it	Very often use it
Entire sample	6,67%	11,67%	31,67%	28,33%	15,00%	6,67%

Table 3.16.2 How often do you use Google Earth? Broken out by Population size of the area served

Population size of the area served	No Answer	Never really use it	Seldom use it	Sometimes use it	Often Use it	Very often use it
Less than 2000	14,29%	14,29%	21,43%	42,86%	7,14%	0,00%
2000 - 10000	0,00%	0,00%	40,00%	26,67%	13,33%	20,00%
10000+ - 45000	0,00%	6,67%	33,33%	33,33%	26,67%	0,00%
More than 45000	12,50%	25,00%	31,25%	12,50%	12,50%	6,25%

Table 3.16.3 How often do you use Google Earth? Broken out by Age range of survey participant

Age range of survey participant	No Answer	Never really use it	Seldom use it	Sometimes use it	Often Use it	Very often use it
Under 30	0,00%	66,67%	0,00%	0,00%	33,33%	0,00%
30-39	0,00%	0,00%	28,57%	28,57%	42,86%	0,00%
40-49	0,00%	0,00%	50,00%	33,33%	0,00%	16,67%
50-59	8,00%	16,00%	28,00%	28,00%	12,00%	8,00%
60-69	10,00%	10,00%	30,00%	30,00%	20,00%	0,00%
70 or Over	33,33%	0,00%	33,33%	33,33%	0,00%	0,00%

Table 3.16.4 How often do you use Google Earth? Broken out by Library's annual budget, $

Library's annual budget, $	No Answer	Never really use it	Seldom use it	Sometimes use it	Often Use it	Very often use it
Less than 50000	13,33%	13,33%	33,33%	33,33%	6,67%	0,00%
50000 - 300000	0,00%	6,25%	31,25%	31,25%	18,75%	12,50%
300000+ - 1500000	13,33%	6,67%	26,67%	33,33%	13,33%	6,67%
More than 1500000	0,00%	21,43%	35,71%	14,29%	21,43%	7,14%

Table 3.16.5 How often do you use Google Earth? Broken out by Gender of survey participant

Gender of survey participant	No Answer	Never really use it	Seldom use it	Sometimes use it	Often Use it	Very often use it
Male	0,00%	0,00%	60,00%	20,00%	20,00%	0,00%
Female	7,27%	12,73%	29,09%	29,09%	14,55%	7,27%

Table 3.17.1 How often do you use Google Sky?

	No Answer	Never really use it	Seldom use it	Sometimes use it	Often Use it	Very often use it
Entire sample	3,33%	65,00%	16,67%	10,00%	5,00%	0,00%

Table 3.17.2 How often do you use Google Sky? Broken out by Population size of the area served

Population size of the area served	No Answer	Never really use it	Seldom use it	Sometimes use it	Often Use it	Very often use it
Less than 2000	0,00%	71,43%	14,29%	7,14%	7,14%	0,00%
2000 - 10000	13,33%	66,67%	13,33%	6,67%	0,00%	0,00%
10000+ - 45000	0,00%	46,67%	26,67%	20,00%	6,67%	0,00%
More than 45000	0,00%	75,00%	12,50%	6,25%	6,25%	0,00%

Table 3.17.3 How often do you use Google Sky? Broken out by Age range of survey participant

Age range of survey participant	No Answer	Never really use it	Seldom use it	Sometimes use it	Often Use it	Very often use it
Under 30	0,00%	66,67%	33,33%	0,00%	0,00%	0,00%
30-39	0,00%	57,14%	14,29%	14,29%	14,29%	0,00%
40-49	8,33%	41,67%	41,67%	8,33%	0,00%	0,00%
50-59	0,00%	84,00%	8,00%	4,00%	4,00%	0,00%
60-69	10,00%	60,00%	0,00%	20,00%	10,00%	0,00%
70 or Over	0,00%	33,33%	33,33%	33,33%	0,00%	0,00%

Table 3.17.4 How often do you use Google Sky? Broken out by Library's annual budget, $

Library's annual budget, $	No Answer	Never really use it	Seldom use it	Sometimes use it	Often Use it	Very often use it
Less than 50000	0,00%	73,33%	13,33%	6,67%	6,67%	0,00%
50000 - 300000	12,50%	68,75%	6,25%	12,50%	0,00%	0,00%
300000+ - 1500000	0,00%	53,33%	26,67%	13,33%	6,67%	0,00%
More than 1500000	0,00%	64,29%	21,43%	7,14%	7,14%	0,00%

Table 3.17.5 How often do you use Google Sky? Broken out by Gender of survey participant

Gender of survey participant	No Answer	Never really use it	Seldom use it	Sometimes use it	Often Use it	Very often use it
Male	0,00%	60,00%	20,00%	20,00%	0,00%	0,00%
Female	3,64%	65,45%	16,36%	9,09%	5,45%	0,00%

Table 3.18.1 How often do you use Google+?

	Never really use it	Seldom use it	Sometimes use it	Often Use it	Very often use it
Entire sample	56,67%	23,33%	11,67%	3,33%	5,00%

Table 3.18.2 How often do you use Google+? Broken out by Population size of the area served

Population size of the area served	Never really use it	Seldom use it	Sometimes use it	Often Use it	Very often use it
Less than 2000	64,29%	14,29%	14,29%	7,14%	0,00%
2000 - 10000	60,00%	20,00%	13,33%	0,00%	6,67%
10000+ - 45000	46,67%	33,33%	6,67%	0,00%	13,33%
More than 45000	56,25%	25,00%	12,50%	6,25%	0,00%

Table 3.18.3 How often do you use Google+? Broken out by Age range of survey participant

Age range of survey participant	Never really use it	Seldom use it	Sometimes use it	Often Use it	Very often use it
Under 30	100,00%	0,00%	0,00%	0,00%	0,00%
30-39	28,57%	28,57%	14,29%	14,29%	14,29%
40-49	50,00%	25,00%	25,00%	0,00%	0,00%
50-59	64,00%	20,00%	4,00%	4,00%	8,00%
60-69	60,00%	30,00%	10,00%	0,00%	0,00%
70 or Over	33,33%	33,33%	33,33%	0,00%	0,00%

Table 3.18.4 How often do you use Google+? Broken out by Library's annual budget, $

Library's annual budget, $	Never really use it	Seldom use it	Sometimes use it	Often Use it	Very often use it
Less than 50000	66,67%	6,67%	13,33%	13,33%	0,00%
50000 - 300000	50,00%	25,00%	12,50%	0,00%	12,50%
300000+ - 1500000	60,00%	26,67%	6,67%	0,00%	6,67%
More than 1500000	50,00%	35,71%	14,29%	0,00%	0,00%

Table 3.18.5 How often do you use Google+? Broken out by Gender of survey participant

Gender of survey participant	Never really use it	Seldom use it	Sometimes use it	Often Use it	Very often use it
Male	60,00%	20,00%	0,00%	0,00%	20,00%
Female	56,36%	23,64%	12,73%	3,64%	3,64%

Table 3.19.1 How often do you use Google Hangouts?

	Never really use it	Seldom use it	Sometimes use it	Often Use it	Very often use it
Entire sample	56,67%	20,00%	11,67%	6,67%	5,00%

Table 3.19.2 How often do you use Google Hangouts? Broken out by Population size of the area served

Population size of the area served	Never really use it	Seldom use it	Sometimes use it	Often Use it	Very often use it
Less than 2000	71,43%	14,29%	7,14%	0,00%	7,14%
2000 - 10000	46,67%	6,67%	20,00%	20,00%	6,67%
10000+ - 45000	46,67%	33,33%	13,33%	6,67%	0,00%
More than 45000	62,50%	25,00%	6,25%	0,00%	6,25%

Table 3.19.3 How often do you use Google Hangouts? Broken out by Age range of survey participant

Age range of survey participant	Never really use it	Seldom use it	Sometimes use it	Often Use it	Very often use it
Under 30	100,00%	0,00%	0,00%	0,00%	0,00%
30-39	0,00%	14,29%	28,57%	28,57%	28,57%
40-49	50,00%	33,33%	8,33%	8,33%	0,00%
50-59	64,00%	16,00%	12,00%	4,00%	4,00%
60-69	60,00%	30,00%	10,00%	0,00%	0,00%
70 or Over	100,00%	0,00%	0,00%	0,00%	0,00%

Table 3.19.4 How often do you use Google Hangouts? Broken out by Library's annual budget, $

Library's annual budget, $	Never really use it	Seldom use it	Sometimes use it	Often Use it	Very often use it
Less than 50000	86,67%	6,67%	6,67%	0,00%	0,00%
50000 - 300000	43,75%	18,75%	6,25%	25,00%	6,25%
300000+ - 1500000	40,00%	33,33%	13,33%	0,00%	13,33%
More than 1500000	57,14%	21,43%	21,43%	0,00%	0,00%

Table 3.19.5 How often do you use Google Hangouts? Broken out by Gender of survey participant

Gender of survey participant	Never really use it	Seldom use it	Sometimes use it	Often Use it	Very often use it
Male	40,00%	0,00%	20,00%	20,00%	20,00%
Female	58,18%	21,82%	10,91%	5,45%	3,64%

Table 3.20.1 How often do you use Google Bookmarks?

	Never really use it	Seldom use it	Sometimes use it	Often Use it	Very often use it
Entire sample	61,67%	15,00%	10,00%	6,67%	6,67%

Table 3.20.2 How often do you use Google Bookmarks? Broken out by Population size of the area served

Population size of the area served	Never really use it	Seldom use it	Sometimes use it	Often Use it	Very often use it
Less than 2000	71,43%	14,29%	14,29%	0,00%	0,00%
2000 - 10000	60,00%	6,67%	0,00%	13,33%	20,00%
10000+ - 45000	46,67%	33,33%	6,67%	6,67%	6,67%
More than 45000	68,75%	6,25%	18,75%	6,25%	0,00%

Table 3.20.3 How often do you use Google Bookmarks? Broken out by Age range of survey participant

Age range of survey participant	Never really use it	Seldom use it	Sometimes use it	Often Use it	Very often use it
Under 30	66,67%	0,00%	0,00%	0,00%	33,33%
30-39	14,29%	14,29%	57,14%	0,00%	14,29%
40-49	58,33%	16,67%	8,33%	8,33%	8,33%
50-59	72,00%	12,00%	0,00%	12,00%	4,00%
60-69	70,00%	20,00%	10,00%	0,00%	0,00%
70 or Over	66,67%	33,33%	0,00%	0,00%	0,00%

Table 3.20.4 How often do you use Google Bookmarks? Broken out by Library's annual budget, $

Library's annual budget, $	Never really use it	Seldom use it	Sometimes use it	Often Use it	Very often use it
Less than 50000	80,00%	6,67%	13,33%	0,00%	0,00%
50000 - 300000	56,25%	18,75%	6,25%	6,25%	12,50%
300000+ - 1500000	46,67%	20,00%	6,67%	13,33%	13,33%
More than 1500000	64,29%	14,29%	14,29%	7,14%	0,00%

Table 3.20.5 How often do you use Google Bookmarks? Broken out by Gender of survey participant

Gender of survey participant	Never really use it	Seldom use it	Sometimes use it	Often Use it	Very often use it
Male	40,00%	20,00%	40,00%	0,00%	0,00%
Female	63,64%	14,55%	7,27%	7,27%	7,27%

Table 3.21.1 How often do you use Google Patent Search?

	Never really use it	Seldom use it	Sometimes use it	Often Use it	Very often use it
Entire sample	83,33%	10,00%	6,67%	0,00%	0,00%

Table 3.21.2 How often do you use Google Patent Search? Broken out by Population size of the area served

Population size of the area served	Never really use it	Seldom use it	Sometimes use it	Often Use it	Very often use it
Less than 2000	92,86%	0,00%	7,14%	0,00%	0,00%
2000 - 10000	80,00%	13,33%	6,67%	0,00%	0,00%
10000+ - 45000	86,67%	6,67%	6,67%	0,00%	0,00%
More than 45000	75,00%	18,75%	6,25%	0,00%	0,00%

Table 3.21.3 How often do you use Google Patent Search? Broken out by Age range of survey participant

Age range of survey participant	Never really use it	Seldom use it	Sometimes use it	Often Use it	Very often use it
Under 30	100,00%	0,00%	0,00%	0,00%	0,00%
30-39	71,43%	14,29%	14,29%	0,00%	0,00%
40-49	58,33%	33,33%	8,33%	0,00%	0,00%
50-59	96,00%	0,00%	4,00%	0,00%	0,00%
60-69	80,00%	10,00%	10,00%	0,00%	0,00%
70 or Over	100,00%	0,00%	0,00%	0,00%	0,00%

Table 3.21.4 How often do you use Google Patent Search? Broken out by Library's annual budget, $

Library's annual budget, $	Never really use it	Seldom use it	Sometimes use it	Often Use it	Very often use it
Less than 50000	86,67%	0,00%	13,33%	0,00%	0,00%
50000 - 300000	87,50%	0,00%	12,50%	0,00%	0,00%
300000+ - 1500000	73,33%	26,67%	0,00%	0,00%	0,00%
More than 1500000	85,71%	14,29%	0,00%	0,00%	0,00%

Table 3.21.5 How often do you use Google Patent Search? Broken out by Gender of survey participant

Gender of survey participant	Never really use it	Seldom use it	Sometimes use it	Often Use it	Very often use it
Male	80,00%	20,00%	0,00%	0,00%	0,00%
Female	83,64%	9,09%	7,27%	0,00%	0,00%

Table 3.22.1 How often do you use Google Forms?

	No Answer	Never really use it	Seldom use it	Sometimes use it	Often Use it	Very often use it
Entire sample	1,67%	50,00%	20,00%	16,67%	8,33%	3,33%

Table 3.22.2 How often do you use Google Forms? Broken out by Population size of the area served

Population size of the area served	No Answer	Never really use it	Seldom use it	Sometimes use it	Often Use it	Very often use it
Less than 2000	0,00%	71,43%	7,14%	21,43%	0,00%	0,00%
2000 - 10000	0,00%	40,00%	13,33%	20,00%	13,33%	13,33%
10000+ - 45000	0,00%	40,00%	40,00%	13,33%	6,67%	0,00%
More than 45000	6,25%	50,00%	18,75%	12,50%	12,50%	0,00%

Table 3.22.3 How often do you use Google Forms? Broken out by Age range of survey participant

Age range of survey participant	No Answer	Never really use it	Seldom use it	Sometimes use it	Often Use it	Very often use it
Under 30	0,00%	66,67%	0,00%	0,00%	33,33%	0,00%
30-39	0,00%	14,29%	14,29%	71,43%	0,00%	0,00%
40-49	0,00%	33,33%	25,00%	16,67%	8,33%	16,67%
50-59	4,00%	64,00%	12,00%	12,00%	8,00%	0,00%
60-69	0,00%	40,00%	50,00%	0,00%	10,00%	0,00%
70 or Over	0,00%	100,00%	0,00%	0,00%	0,00%	0,00%

Table 3.22.4 How often do you use Google Forms? Broken out by Library's annual budget, $

Library's annual budget, $	No Answer	Never really use it	Seldom use it	Sometimes use it	Often Use it	Very often use it
Less than 50000	0,00%	60,00%	6,67%	26,67%	6,67%	0,00%
50000 - 300000	0,00%	56,25%	18,75%	12,50%	6,25%	6,25%
300000+ - 1500000	6,67%	40,00%	20,00%	20,00%	6,67%	6,67%
More than 1500000	0,00%	42,86%	35,71%	7,14%	14,29%	0,00%

Table 3.22.5 How often do you use Google Forms? Broken out by Gender of survey participant

Gender of survey participant	No Answer	Never really use it	Seldom use it	Sometimes use it	Often Use it	Very often use it
Male	0,00%	40,00%	20,00%	40,00%	0,00%	0,00%
Female	1,82%	50,91%	20,00%	14,55%	9,09%	3,64%

Table 3.23.1 How often do you use Google Slides?

	No Answer	Never really use it	Seldom use it	Sometimes use it	Often Use it	Very often use it
Entire sample	3,33%	66,67%	15,00%	13,33%	1,67%	0,00%

Table 3.23.2 How often do you use Google Slides? Broken out by Population size of the area served

Population size of the area served	No Answer	Never really use it	Seldom use it	Sometimes use it	Often Use it	Very often use it
Less than 2000	7,14%	78,57%	0,00%	14,29%	0,00%	0,00%
2000 - 10000	0,00%	66,67%	20,00%	13,33%	0,00%	0,00%
10000+ - 45000	6,67%	60,00%	20,00%	13,33%	0,00%	0,00%
More than 45000	0,00%	62,50%	18,75%	12,50%	6,25%	0,00%

Table 3.23.3 How often do you use Google Slides? Broken out by Age range of survey participant

Age range of survey participant	No Answer	Never really use it	Seldom use it	Sometimes use it	Often Use it	Very often use it
Under 30	0,00%	66,67%	0,00%	0,00%	33,33%	0,00%
30-39	0,00%	28,57%	14,29%	57,14%	0,00%	0,00%
40-49	0,00%	50,00%	33,33%	16,67%	0,00%	0,00%
50-59	4,00%	88,00%	8,00%	0,00%	0,00%	0,00%
60-69	10,00%	50,00%	20,00%	20,00%	0,00%	0,00%
70 or Over	0,00%	100,00%	0,00%	0,00%	0,00%	0,00%

Table 3.23.4 How often do you use Google Slides? Broken out by Library's annual budget, $

Library's annual budget, $	No Answer	Never really use it	Seldom use it	Sometimes use it	Often Use it	Very often use it
Less than 50000	6,67%	66,67%	0,00%	26,67%	0,00%	0,00%
50000 - 300000	0,00%	81,25%	6,25%	12,50%	0,00%	0,00%
300000+ - 1500000	0,00%	60,00%	33,33%	6,67%	0,00%	0,00%
More than 1500000	7,14%	57,14%	21,43%	7,14%	7,14%	0,00%

Table 3.23.5 How often do you use Google Slides? Broken out by Gender of survey participant

Gender of survey participant	No Answer	Never really use it	Seldom use it	Sometimes use it	Often Use it	Very often use it
Male	0,00%	60,00%	20,00%	20,00%	0,00%	0,00%
Female	3,64%	67,27%	14,55%	12,73%	1,82%	0,00%

Table 3.24.1 How often do you use Google Groups?

	No Answer	Never really use it	Seldom use it	Sometimes use it	Often Use it	Very often use it
Entire sample	1,67%	63,33%	18,33%	13,33%	1,67%	1,67%

Table 3.24.2 How often do you use Google Groups? Broken out by Population size of the area served

Population size of the area served	No Answer	Never really use it	Seldom use it	Sometimes use it	Often Use it	Very often use it
Less than 2000	0,00%	78,57%	7,14%	14,29%	0,00%	0,00%
2000 - 10000	0,00%	73,33%	6,67%	13,33%	0,00%	6,67%
10000+ - 45000	0,00%	46,67%	40,00%	6,67%	6,67%	0,00%
More than 45000	6,25%	56,25%	18,75%	18,75%	0,00%	0,00%

Table 3.24.3 How often do you use Google Groups? Broken out by Age range of survey participant

Age range of survey participant	No Answer	Never really use it	Seldom use it	Sometimes use it	Often Use it	Very often use it
Under 30	0,00%	100,00%	0,00%	0,00%	0,00%	0,00%
30-39	0,00%	14,29%	28,57%	42,86%	14,29%	0,00%
40-49	0,00%	58,33%	25,00%	8,33%	0,00%	8,33%
50-59	4,00%	76,00%	12,00%	8,00%	0,00%	0,00%
60-69	0,00%	50,00%	30,00%	20,00%	0,00%	0,00%
70 or Over	0,00%	100,00%	0,00%	0,00%	0,00%	0,00%

Table 3.24.4 How often do you use Google Groups? Broken out by Library's annual budget, $

Library's annual budget, $	No Answer	Never really use it	Seldom use it	Sometimes use it	Often Use it	Very often use it
Less than 50000	0,00%	80,00%	6,67%	13,33%	0,00%	0,00%
50000 - 300000	0,00%	62,50%	25,00%	6,25%	6,25%	0,00%
300000+ - 1500000	6,67%	60,00%	20,00%	6,67%	0,00%	6,67%
More than 1500000	0,00%	50,00%	21,43%	28,57%	0,00%	0,00%

Table 3.24.5 How often do you use Google Groups? Broken out by Gender of survey participant

Gender of survey participant	No Answer	Never really use it	Seldom use it	Sometimes use it	Often Use it	Very often use it
Male	0,00%	40,00%	40,00%	0,00%	20,00%	0,00%
Female	1,82%	65,45%	16,36%	14,55%	0,00%	1,82%

Table 3.25.1 How often do you use Google Analytics?

	Never really use it	Seldom use it	Sometimes use it	Often Use it	Very often use it
Entire sample	56,67%	16,67%	11,67%	10,00%	5,00%

Table 3.25.2 How often do you use Google Analytics? Broken out by Population size of the area served

Population size of the area served	Never really use it	Seldom use it	Sometimes use it	Often Use it	Very often use it
Less than 2000	85,71%	0,00%	7,14%	7,14%	0,00%
2000 - 10000	73,33%	6,67%	13,33%	6,67%	0,00%
10000+ - 45000	33,33%	46,67%	6,67%	6,67%	6,67%
More than 45000	37,50%	12,50%	18,75%	18,75%	12,50%

Table 3.25.3 How often do you use Google Analytics? Broken out by Age range of survey participant

Age range of survey participant	Never really use it	Seldom use it	Sometimes use it	Often Use it	Very often use it
Under 30	66,67%	33,33%	0,00%	0,00%	0,00%
30-39	28,57%	14,29%	14,29%	28,57%	14,29%
40-49	41,67%	8,33%	16,67%	16,67%	16,67%
50-59	68,00%	8,00%	16,00%	8,00%	0,00%
60-69	50,00%	50,00%	0,00%	0,00%	0,00%
70 or Over	100,00%	0,00%	0,00%	0,00%	0,00%

Table 3.25.4 How often do you use Google Analytics? Broken out by Library's annual budget, $

Library's annual budget, $	Never really use it	Seldom use it	Sometimes use it	Often Use it	Very often use it
Less than 50000	80,00%	6,67%	6,67%	6,67%	0,00%
50000 - 300000	75,00%	12,50%	6,25%	0,00%	6,25%
300000+ - 1500000	20,00%	40,00%	26,67%	13,33%	0,00%
More than 1500000	50,00%	7,14%	7,14%	21,43%	14,29%

Table 3.25.5 How often do you use Google Analytics? Broken out by Gender of survey participant

Gender of survey participant	Never really use it	Seldom use it	Sometimes use it	Often Use it	Very often use it
Male	40,00%	20,00%	0,00%	20,00%	20,00%
Female	58,18%	16,36%	12,73%	9,09%	3,64%

Table 3.26.1 How often do you use AdWords?

	No Answer	Never really use it	Seldom use it	Sometimes use it	Often Use it	Very often use it
Entire sample	3,33%	86,67%	8,33%	1,67%	0,00%	0,00%

Table 3.26.2 How often do you use AdWords? Broken out by Population size of the area served

Population size of the area served	No Answer	Never really use it	Seldom use it	Sometimes use it	Often Use it	Very often use it
Less than 2000	0,00%	92,86%	7,14%	0,00%	0,00%	0,00%
2000 - 10000	0,00%	86,67%	6,67%	6,67%	0,00%	0,00%
10000+ - 45000	0,00%	86,67%	13,33%	0,00%	0,00%	0,00%
More than 45000	12,50%	81,25%	6,25%	0,00%	0,00%	0,00%

Table 3.26.3 How often do you use AdWords? Broken out by Age range of survey participant

Age range of survey participant	No Answer	Never really use it	Seldom use it	Sometimes use it	Often Use it	Very often use it
Under 30	0,00%	100,00%	0,00%	0,00%	0,00%	0,00%
30-39	0,00%	85,71%	14,29%	0,00%	0,00%	0,00%
40-49	0,00%	75,00%	16,67%	8,33%	0,00%	0,00%
50-59	8,00%	92,00%	0,00%	0,00%	0,00%	0,00%
60-69	0,00%	80,00%	20,00%	0,00%	0,00%	0,00%
70 or Over	0,00%	100,00%	0,00%	0,00%	0,00%	0,00%

Table 3.26.4 How often do you use AdWords? Broken out by Library's annual budget, $

Library's annual budget, $	No Answer	Never really use it	Seldom use it	Sometimes use it	Often Use it	Very often use it
Less than 50000	0,00%	86,67%	13,33%	0,00%	0,00%	0,00%
50000 - 300000	0,00%	87,50%	6,25%	6,25%	0,00%	0,00%
300000+ - 1500000	6,67%	86,67%	6,67%	0,00%	0,00%	0,00%
More than 1500000	7,14%	85,71%	7,14%	0,00%	0,00%	0,00%

Table 3.26.5 How often do you use AdWords? Broken out by Gender of survey participant

Gender of survey participant	No Answer	Never really use it	Seldom use it	Sometimes use it	Often Use it	Very often use it
Male	0,00%	100,00%	0,00%	0,00%	0,00%	0,00%
Female	3,64%	85,45%	9,09%	1,82%	0,00%	0,00%

Table 3.27.1 How often do you use AdSense?

	Never really use it	Seldom use it	Sometimes use it	Often Use it	Very often use it
Entire sample	88,33%	10,00%	1,67%	0,00%	0,00%

Table 3.27.2 How often do you use AdSense? Broken out by Population size of the area served

Population size of the area served	Never really use it	Seldom use it	Sometimes use it	Often Use it	Very often use it
Less than 2000	92,86%	7,14%	0,00%	0,00%	0,00%
2000 - 10000	86,67%	6,67%	6,67%	0,00%	0,00%
10000+ - 45000	86,67%	13,33%	0,00%	0,00%	0,00%
More than 45000	87,50%	12,50%	0,00%	0,00%	0,00%

Table 3.27.3 How often do you use AdSense? Broken out by Age range of survey participant

Age range of survey participant	Never really use it	Seldom use it	Sometimes use it	Often Use it	Very often use it
Under 30	100,00%	0,00%	0,00%	0,00%	0,00%
30-39	85,71%	14,29%	0,00%	0,00%	0,00%
40-49	75,00%	16,67%	8,33%	0,00%	0,00%
50-59	96,00%	4,00%	0,00%	0,00%	0,00%
60-69	80,00%	20,00%	0,00%	0,00%	0,00%

70 or Over	100,00%	0,00%	0,00%	0,00%	0,00%

Table 3.27.4 How often do you use AdSense? Broken out by Library's annual budget, $

Library's annual budget, $	Never really use it	Seldom use it	Sometimes use it	Often Use it	Very often use it
Less than 50000	86,67%	13,33%	0,00%	0,00%	0,00%
50000 - 300000	87,50%	6,25%	6,25%	0,00%	0,00%
300000+ - 1500000	86,67%	13,33%	0,00%	0,00%	0,00%
More than 1500000	92,86%	7,14%	0,00%	0,00%	0,00%

Table 3.27.5 How often do you use AdSense? Broken out by Gender of survey participant

Gender of survey participant	Never really use it	Seldom use it	Sometimes use it	Often Use it	Very often use it
Male	100,00%	0,00%	0,00%	0,00%	0,00%
Female	87,27%	10,91%	1,82%	0,00%	0,00%

Table 3.28.1 How often do you use Blogger?

	No Answer	Never really use it	Seldom use it	Sometimes use it	Often Use it	Very often use it
Entire sample	1,67%	76,67%	11,67%	5,00%	1,67%	3,33%

Table 3.28.2 How often do you use Blogger? Broken out by Population size of the area served

Population size of the area served	No Answer	Never really use it	Seldom use it	Sometimes use it	Often Use it	Very often use it
Less than 2000	0,00%	85,71%	14,29%	0,00%	0,00%	0,00%
2000 - 10000	6,67%	66,67%	6,67%	6,67%	6,67%	6,67%
10000+ - 45000	0,00%	80,00%	6,67%	6,67%	0,00%	6,67%
More than 45000	0,00%	75,00%	18,75%	6,25%	0,00%	0,00%

Table 3.28.3 How often do you use Blogger? Broken out by Age range of survey participant

Age range of survey participant	No Answer	Never really use it	Seldom use it	Sometimes use it	Often Use it	Very often use it
Under 30	0,00%	33,33%	33,33%	0,00%	0,00%	33,33%
30-39	0,00%	71,43%	14,29%	14,29%	0,00%	0,00%
40-49	8,33%	41,67%	16,67%	16,67%	8,33%	8,33%
50-59	0,00%	100,00%	0,00%	0,00%	0,00%	0,00%
60-69	0,00%	80,00%	20,00%	0,00%	0,00%	0,00%
70 or Over	0,00%	66,67%	33,33%	0,00%	0,00%	0,00%

Table 3.28.4 How often do you use Blogger? Broken out by Library's annual budget, $

Library's annual budget, $	No Answer	Never really use it	Seldom use it	Sometimes use it	Often Use it	Very often use it
Less than 50000	0,00%	86,67%	13,33%	0,00%	0,00%	0,00%
50000 - 300000	6,25%	75,00%	6,25%	6,25%	0,00%	6,25%
300000+ - 1500000	0,00%	73,33%	6,67%	6,67%	6,67%	6,67%
More than 1500000	0,00%	71,43%	21,43%	7,14%	0,00%	0,00%

Table 3.28.5 How often do you use Blogger? Broken out by Gender of survey participant

Gender of survey participant	No Answer	Never really use it	Seldom use it	Sometimes use it	Often Use it	Very often use it
Male	0,00%	100,00%	0,00%	0,00%	0,00%	0,00%
Female	1,82%	74,55%	12,73%	5,45%	1,82%	3,64%

Table 3.29.1 How often do you use YouTube?

	Never really use it	Seldom use it	Sometimes use it	Often Use it	Very often use it
Entire sample	10,00%	18,33%	31,67%	25,00%	15,00%

Table 3.29.2 How often do you use YouTube? Broken out by Population size of the area served

Population size of the area served	Never really use it	Seldom use it	Sometimes use it	Often Use it	Very often use it
Less than 2000	7,14%	35,71%	21,43%	28,57%	7,14%
2000 - 10000	13,33%	13,33%	46,67%	13,33%	13,33%
10000+ - 45000	20,00%	13,33%	26,67%	20,00%	20,00%
More than 45000	0,00%	12,50%	31,25%	37,50%	18,75%

Table 3.29.3 How often do you use YouTube? Broken out by Age range of survey participant

Age range of survey participant	Never really use it	Seldom use it	Sometimes use it	Often Use it	Very often use it
Under 30	0,00%	33,33%	0,00%	33,33%	33,33%
30-39	0,00%	14,29%	28,57%	42,86%	14,29%
40-49	33,33%	25,00%	16,67%	8,33%	16,67%
50-59	0,00%	8,00%	44,00%	32,00%	16,00%
60-69	20,00%	20,00%	30,00%	20,00%	10,00%
70 or Over	0,00%	66,67%	33,33%	0,00%	0,00%

Table 3.29.4 How often do you use YouTube? Broken out by Library's annual budget, $

Library's annual budget, $	Never really use it	Seldom use it	Sometimes use it	Often Use it	Very often use it
Less than 50000	13,33%	26,67%	20,00%	33,33%	6,67%
50000 - 300000	6,25%	12,50%	50,00%	12,50%	18,75%
300000+ - 1500000	13,33%	20,00%	33,33%	13,33%	20,00%
More than 1500000	7,14%	14,29%	21,43%	42,86%	14,29%

Table 3.29.5 How often do you use YouTube? Broken out by Gender of survey participant

Gender of survey participant	Never really use it	Seldom use it	Sometimes use it	Often Use it	Very often use it
Male	20,00%	0,00%	60,00%	0,00%	20,00%
Female	9,09%	20,00%	29,09%	27,27%	14,55%

Table 4 When you do use the following features of Google how useful are they to you?

Table 4.1.1 When you do use Google Maps how useful are they to you?

	Don't use this at all	Not very useful	Somewhat useful	Useful	Quite useful
Entire sample	3,33%	10,00%	15,00%	38,33%	33,33%

Table 4.1.2 When you do use Google Maps how useful are they to you? Broken out by Population size of the area served

Population size of the area served	Don't use this at all	Not very useful	Somewhat useful	Useful	Quite useful
Less than 2000	0,00%	21,43%	14,29%	50,00%	14,29%
2000 - 10000	0,00%	6,67%	20,00%	33,33%	40,00%
10000+ - 45000	6,67%	13,33%	6,67%	26,67%	46,67%
More than 45000	6,25%	0,00%	18,75%	43,75%	31,25%

Table 4.1.3 When you do use Google Maps how useful are they to you? Broken out by Age range of survey participant

Age range of survey participant	Don't use this at all	Not very useful	Somewhat useful	Useful	Quite useful
Under 30	0,00%	0,00%	0,00%	33,33%	66,67%
30-39	0,00%	0,00%	0,00%	57,14%	42,86%
40-49	0,00%	0,00%	8,33%	58,33%	33,33%
50-59	4,00%	12,00%	20,00%	28,00%	36,00%
60-69	10,00%	20,00%	20,00%	30,00%	20,00%
70 or Over	0,00%	33,33%	33,33%	33,33%	0,00%

Table 4.1.4 When you do use Google Maps how useful are they to you? Broken out by Library's annual budget, $

Library's annual budget, $	Don't use this at all	Not very useful	Somewhat useful	Useful	Quite useful
Less than 50000	6,67%	6,67%	26,67%	40,00%	20,00%
50000 - 300000	6,25%	25,00%	12,50%	18,75%	37,50%
300000+ - 1500000	0,00%	6,67%	13,33%	53,33%	26,67%
More than 1500000	0,00%	0,00%	7,14%	42,86%	50,00%

Table 4.1.5 When you do use Google Maps how useful are they to you? Broken out by Gender of survey participant

Gender of survey participant	Don't use this at all	Not very useful	Somewhat useful	Useful	Quite useful
Male	20,00%	0,00%	0,00%	20,00%	60,00%
Female	1,82%	10,91%	16,36%	40,00%	30,91%

Table 4.2.1 When you do use Google Advanced Search how useful are they to you?

	Don't use this at all	Not very useful	Somewhat useful	Useful	Quite useful	Essential
Entire sample	28,33%	1,67%	16,67%	16,67%	25,00%	11,67%

Table 4.2.2 When you do use Google Advanced Search how useful are they to you? Broken out by Population size of the area served

Population size of the area served	Don't use this at all	Not very useful	Somewhat useful	Useful	Quite useful	Essential
Less than 2000	64,29%	0,00%	14,29%	7,14%	7,14%	7,14%
2000 - 10000	20,00%	0,00%	20,00%	26,67%	26,67%	6,67%
10000+ - 45000	20,00%	6,67%	26,67%	13,33%	26,67%	6,67%
More than 45000	12,50%	0,00%	6,25%	18,75%	37,50%	25,00%

Table 4.2.3 When you do use Google Advanced Search how useful are they to you? Broken out by Age range of survey participant

Age range of survey participant	Don't use this at all	Not very useful	Somewhat useful	Useful	Quite useful	Essential
Under 30	0,00%	0,00%	33,33%	0,00%	33,33%	33,33%
30-39	14,29%	0,00%	14,29%	0,00%	42,86%	28,57%
40-49	25,00%	0,00%	8,33%	33,33%	25,00%	8,33%
50-59	36,00%	0,00%	20,00%	16,00%	20,00%	8,00%
60-69	20,00%	10,00%	20,00%	10,00%	30,00%	10,00%
70 or Over	66,67%	0,00%	0,00%	33,33%	0,00%	0,00%

Table 4.2.4 When you do use Google Advanced Search how useful are they to you? Broken out by Library's annual budget, $

Library's annual budget, $	Don't use this at all	Not very useful	Somewhat useful	Useful	Quite useful	Essential
Less than 50000	53,33%	0,00%	13,33%	13,33%	13,33%	6,67%
50000 - 300000	18,75%	6,25%	25,00%	18,75%	25,00%	6,25%
300000+ - 1500000	13,33%	0,00%	13,33%	26,67%	40,00%	6,67%
More than 1500000	28,57%	0,00%	14,29%	7,14%	21,43%	28,57%

Table 4.2.5 When you do use Google Advanced Search how useful are they to you? Broken out by Gender of survey participant

Gender of survey participant	Don't use this at all	Not very useful	Somewhat useful	Useful	Quite useful	Essential
Male	0,00%	0,00%	40,00%	0,00%	40,00%	20,00%
Female	30,91%	1,82%	14,55%	18,18%	23,64%	10,91%

Table 4.3.1 When you do use Google Alerts how useful are they to you?

	No Answer	Don't use this at all	Not very useful	Somewhat useful	Useful	Quite useful	Essential
Entire sample	5,00%	51,67%	3,33%	10,00%	20,00%	8,33%	1,67%

Table 4.3.2 When you do use Google Alerts how useful are they to you? Broken out by Population size of the area served

Population size of the area served	No Answer	Don't use this at all	Not very useful	Somewhat useful	Useful	Quite useful	Essential
Less than 2000	0,00%	71,43%	7,14%	0,00%	14,29%	7,14%	0,00%
2000 - 10000	6,67%	40,00%	0,00%	13,33%	40,00%	0,00%	0,00%
10000+ - 45000	0,00%	53,33%	6,67%	13,33%	6,67%	13,33%	6,67%
More than 45000	12,50%	43,75%	0,00%	12,50%	18,75%	12,50%	0,00%

Table 4.3.3 When you do use Google Alerts how useful are they to you? Broken out by Age range of survey participant

Age range of survey participant	No Answer	Don't use this at all	Not very useful	Somewhat useful	Useful	Quite useful	Essential
Under 30	0,00%	66,67%	0,00%	33,33%	0,00%	0,00%	0,00%
30-39	0,00%	28,57%	14,29%	14,29%	28,57%	14,29%	0,00%
40-49	0,00%	33,33%	0,00%	16,67%	33,33%	16,67%	0,00%
50-59	12,00%	64,00%	0,00%	4,00%	8,00%	8,00%	4,00%
60-69	0,00%	50,00%	0,00%	10,00%	40,00%	0,00%	0,00%
70 or Over	0,00%	66,67%	33,33%	0,00%	0,00%	0,00%	0,00%

Table 4.3.4 When you do use Google Alerts how useful are they to you? Broken out by Library's annual budget, $

Library's annual budget, $	No Answer	Don't use this at all	Not very useful	Somewhat useful	Useful	Quite useful	Essential
Less than 50000	0,00%	73,33%	6,67%	0,00%	13,33%	6,67%	0,00%
50000 - 300000	6,25%	56,25%	0,00%	18,75%	18,75%	0,00%	0,00%
300000+ - 1500000	13,33%	26,67%	0,00%	6,67%	26,67%	20,00%	6,67%
More than 1500000	0,00%	50,00%	7,14%	14,29%	21,43%	7,14%	0,00%

Table 4.3.5 When you do use Google Alerts how useful are they to you? Broken out by Gender of survey participant

Gender of survey participant	No Answer	Don't use this at all	Not very useful	Somewhat useful	Useful	Quite useful	Essential
Male	0,00%	40,00%	20,00%	20,00%	0,00%	20,00%	0,00%
Female	5,45%	52,73%	1,82%	9,09%	21,82%	7,27%	1,82%

Table 4.4.1 When you do use Google Notifications how useful are they to you?

	No Answer	Don't use this at all	Not very useful	Somewhat useful	Useful	Quite useful	Essential
Entire sample	1,67%	51,67%	6,67%	13,33%	16,67%	5,00%	5,00%

Table 4.4.2 When you do use Google Notifications how useful are they to you? Broken out by Population size of the area served

Population size of the area served	No Answer	Don't use this at all	Not very useful	Somewhat useful	Useful	Quite useful	Essential
Less than 2000	0,00%	85,71%	7,14%	7,14%	0,00%	0,00%	0,00%
2000 - 10000	0,00%	40,00%	0,00%	13,33%	33,33%	6,67%	6,67%
10000+ - 45000	0,00%	60,00%	13,33%	0,00%	13,33%	0,00%	13,33%
More than 45000	6,25%	25,00%	6,25%	31,25%	18,75%	12,50%	0,00%

Table 4.4.3 When you do use Google Notifications how useful are they to you? Broken out by Age range of survey participant

Age range of survey participant	No Answer	Don't use this at all	Not very useful	Somewhat useful	Useful	Quite useful	Essential
Under 30	0,00%	33,33%	33,33%	33,33%	0,00%	0,00%	0,00%
30-39	0,00%	28,57%	14,29%	14,29%	28,57%	14,29%	0,00%
40-49	0,00%	33,33%	0,00%	25,00%	33,33%	8,33%	0,00%
50-59	4,00%	60,00%	4,00%	12,00%	4,00%	4,00%	12,00%
60-69	0,00%	60,00%	10,00%	0,00%	30,00%	0,00%	0,00%
70 or Over	0,00%	100,00%	0,00%	0,00%	0,00%	0,00%	0,00%

Table 4.4.4 When you do use Google Notifications how useful are they to you? Broken out by Library's annual budget, $

Library's annual budget, $	No Answer	Don't use this at all	Not very useful	Somewhat useful	Useful	Quite useful	Essential
Less than 50000	0,00%	86,67%	0,00%	6,67%	6,67%	0,00%	0,00%
50000 - 300000	0,00%	50,00%	12,50%	12,50%	18,75%	6,25%	0,00%
300000+ - 1500000	6,67%	40,00%	0,00%	6,67%	20,00%	6,67%	20,00%
More than 1500000	0,00%	28,57%	14,29%	28,57%	21,43%	7,14%	0,00%

Table 4.4.5 When you do use Google Notifications how useful are they to you? Broken out by Gender of survey participant

Gender of survey participant	No Answer	Don't use this at all	Not very useful	Somewhat useful	Useful	Quite useful	Essential
Male	0,00%	40,00%	20,00%	0,00%	20,00%	20,00%	0,00%
Female	1,82%	52,73%	5,45%	14,55%	16,36%	3,64%	5,45%

Table 4.5.1 When you do use Google Images how useful are they to you?

	Don't use this at all	Not very useful	Somewhat useful	Useful	Quite useful	Essential
Entire sample	10,00%	0,00%	8,33%	18,33%	36,67%	26,67%

Table 4.5.2 When you do use Google Images how useful are they to you? Broken out by Population size of the area served

Population size of the area served	Don't use this at all	Not very useful	Somewhat useful	Useful	Quite useful	Essential
Less than 2000	14,29%	0,00%	7,14%	35,71%	35,71%	7,14%
2000 - 10000	20,00%	0,00%	0,00%	20,00%	20,00%	40,00%
10000+ - 45000	6,67%	0,00%	20,00%	13,33%	20,00%	40,00%
More than 45000	0,00%	0,00%	6,25%	6,25%	68,75%	18,75%

Table 4.5.3 When you do use Google Images how useful are they to you? Broken out by Age range of survey participant

Age range of survey participant	Don't use this at all	Not very useful	Somewhat useful	Useful	Quite useful	Essential
Under 30	0,00%	0,00%	0,00%	0,00%	33,33%	66,67%
30-39	0,00%	0,00%	0,00%	0,00%	57,14%	42,86%
40-49	8,33%	0,00%	0,00%	25,00%	33,33%	33,33%
50-59	4,00%	0,00%	8,00%	24,00%	44,00%	20,00%
60-69	30,00%	0,00%	20,00%	10,00%	20,00%	20,00%
70 or Over	33,33%	0,00%	33,33%	33,33%	0,00%	0,00%

Table 4.5.4 When you do use Google Images how useful are they to you? Broken out by Library's annual budget, $

Library's annual budget, $	Don't use this at all	Not very useful	Somewhat useful	Useful	Quite useful	Essential
Less than 50000	26,67%	0,00%	6,67%	26,67%	26,67%	13,33%
50000 - 300000	12,50%	0,00%	6,25%	37,50%	12,50%	31,25%
300000+ - 1500000	0,00%	0,00%	13,33%	6,67%	53,33%	26,67%
More than 1500000	0,00%	0,00%	7,14%	0,00%	57,14%	35,71%

Table 4.5.5 When you do use Google Images how useful are they to you? Broken out by Gender of survey participant

Gender of survey participant	Don't use this at all	Not very useful	Somewhat useful	Useful	Quite useful	Essential
Male	20,00%	0,00%	0,00%	0,00%	40,00%	40,00%
Female	9,09%	0,00%	9,09%	20,00%	36,36%	25,45%

Table 4.6.1 When you do use Google Photos how useful are they to you?

	No Answer	Don't use this at all	Not very useful	Somewhat useful	Useful	Quite useful	Essential
Entire sample	3,33%	35,00%	8,33%	13,33%	15,00%	18,33%	6,67%

Table 4.6.2 When you do use Google Photos how useful are they to you? Broken out by Population size of the area served

Population size of the area served	No Answer	Don't use this at all	Not very useful	Somewhat useful	Useful	Quite useful	Essential
Less than 2000	0,00%	50,00%	7,14%	7,14%	14,29%	21,43%	0,00%
2000 - 10000	0,00%	33,33%	0,00%	6,67%	20,00%	33,33%	6,67%
10000+ - 45000	0,00%	26,67%	13,33%	26,67%	13,33%	0,00%	20,00%
More than 45000	12,50%	31,25%	12,50%	12,50%	12,50%	18,75%	0,00%

Table 4.6.3 When you do use Google Photos how useful are they to you? Broken out by Age range of survey participant

Age range of survey participant	No Answer	Don't use this at all	Not very useful	Somewhat useful	Useful	Quite useful	Essential
Under 30	0,00%	33,33%	33,33%	0,00%	0,00%	0,00%	33,33%
30-39	0,00%	14,29%	0,00%	14,29%	14,29%	57,14%	0,00%
40-49	8,33%	25,00%	8,33%	8,33%	25,00%	25,00%	0,00%
50-59	4,00%	44,00%	8,00%	12,00%	12,00%	8,00%	12,00%
60-69	0,00%	40,00%	10,00%	20,00%	10,00%	20,00%	0,00%
70 or Over	0,00%	33,33%	0,00%	33,33%	33,33%	0,00%	0,00%

Table 4.6.4 When you do use Google Photos how useful are they to you? Broken out by Library's annual budget, $

Library's annual budget, $	No Answer	Don't use this at all	Not very useful	Somewhat useful	Useful	Quite useful	Essential
Less than 50000	0,00%	33,33%	6,67%	6,67%	26,67%	26,67%	0,00%
50000 - 300000	0,00%	43,75%	6,25%	12,50%	18,75%	18,75%	0,00%
300000+ - 1500000	6,67%	26,67%	6,67%	20,00%	0,00%	13,33%	26,67%
More than 1500000	7,14%	35,71%	14,29%	14,29%	14,29%	14,29%	0,00%

Table 4.6.5 When you do use Google Photos how useful are they to you? Broken out by Gender of survey participant

Gender of survey participant	No Answer	Don't use this at all	Not very useful	Somewhat useful	Useful	Quite useful	Essential
Male	0,00%	40,00%	0,00%	20,00%	20,00%	20,00%	0,00%
Female	3,64%	34,55%	9,09%	12,73%	14,55%	18,18%	7,27%

Table 4.7.1 When you do use Google Calendar how useful are they to you?

	No Answer	Don't use this at all	Not very useful	Somewhat useful	Useful	Quite useful	Essential
Entire sample	1,67%	31,67%	6,67%	5,00%	13,33%	11,67%	30,00%

Table 4.7.2 When you do use Google Calendar how useful are they to you? Broken out by Population size of the area served

Population size of the area served	No Answer	Don't use this at all	Not very useful	Somewhat useful	Useful	Quite useful	Essential
Less than 2000	0,00%	42,86%	7,14%	7,14%	14,29%	14,29%	14,29%
2000 - 10000	0,00%	40,00%	0,00%	0,00%	13,33%	6,67%	40,00%
10000+ - 45000	0,00%	13,33%	13,33%	6,67%	20,00%	13,33%	33,33%
More than 45000	6,25%	31,25%	6,25%	6,25%	6,25%	12,50%	31,25%

Table 4.7.3 When you do use Google Calendar how useful are they to you? Broken out by Age range of survey participant

Age range of survey participant	No Answer	Don't use this at all	Not very useful	Somewhat useful	Useful	Quite useful	Essential
Under 30	0,00%	33,33%	0,00%	33,33%	0,00%	0,00%	33,33%
30-39	0,00%	0,00%	0,00%	0,00%	0,00%	28,57%	71,43%
40-49	0,00%	16,67%	8,33%	0,00%	8,33%	16,67%	50,00%
50-59	4,00%	44,00%	0,00%	8,00%	16,00%	4,00%	24,00%
60-69	0,00%	40,00%	20,00%	0,00%	30,00%	10,00%	0,00%
70 or Over	0,00%	33,33%	33,33%	0,00%	0,00%	33,33%	0,00%

Table 4.7.4 When you do use Google Calendar how useful are they to you? Broken out by Library's annual budget, $

Library's annual budget, $	No Answer	Don't use this at all	Not very useful	Somewhat useful	Useful	Quite useful	Essential
Less than 50000	0,00%	46,67%	6,67%	0,00%	20,00%	13,33%	13,33%
50000 - 300000	0,00%	43,75%	6,25%	6,25%	18,75%	6,25%	18,75%
300000+ - 1500000	6,67%	20,00%	6,67%	13,33%	0,00%	6,67%	46,67%
More than 1500000	0,00%	14,29%	7,14%	0,00%	14,29%	21,43%	42,86%

Table 4.7.5 When you do use Google Calendar how useful are they to you? Broken out by Gender of survey participant

Gender of survey participant	No Answer	Don't use this at all	Not very useful	Somewhat useful	Useful	Quite useful	Essential
Male	0,00%	40,00%	0,00%	0,00%	0,00%	20,00%	40,00%
Female	1,82%	30,91%	7,27%	5,45%	14,55%	10,91%	29,09%

Table 4.8.1 When you do use Chrome how useful are they to you?

	No Answer	Don't use this at all	Not very useful	Somewhat useful	Useful	Quite useful	Essential
Entire sample	1,67%	11,67%	5,00%	1,67%	16,67%	25,00%	38,33%

Table 4.8.2 When you do use Chrome how useful are they to you? Broken out by Population size of the area served

Population size of the area served	No Answer	Don't use this at all	Not very useful	Somewhat useful	Useful	Quite useful	Essential
Less than 2000	0,00%	35,71%	7,14%	0,00%	21,43%	21,43%	14,29%
2000 - 10000	0,00%	6,67%	6,67%	0,00%	20,00%	20,00%	46,67%
10000+ - 45000	6,67%	6,67%	6,67%	6,67%	20,00%	13,33%	40,00%
More than 45000	0,00%	0,00%	0,00%	0,00%	6,25%	43,75%	50,00%

Table 4.8.3 When you do use Chrome how useful are they to you? Broken out by Age range of survey participant

Age range of survey participant	No Answer	Don't use this at all	Not very useful	Somewhat useful	Useful	Quite useful	Essential
Under 30	0,00%	0,00%	0,00%	0,00%	0,00%	0,00%	100,00%
30-39	0,00%	0,00%	14,29%	0,00%	0,00%	28,57%	57,14%
40-49	0,00%	16,67%	0,00%	0,00%	8,33%	25,00%	50,00%
50-59	4,00%	8,00%	4,00%	0,00%	16,00%	32,00%	36,00%
60-69	0,00%	20,00%	10,00%	10,00%	30,00%	20,00%	10,00%
70 or Over	0,00%	33,33%	0,00%	0,00%	66,67%	0,00%	0,00%

Table 4.8.4 When you do use Chrome how useful are they to you? Broken out by Library's annual budget, $

Library's annual budget, $	No Answer	Don't use this at all	Not very useful	Somewhat useful	Useful	Quite useful	Essential
Less than 50000	0,00%	26,67%	6,67%	0,00%	40,00%	13,33%	13,33%
50000 - 300000	0,00%	18,75%	6,25%	6,25%	12,50%	18,75%	37,50%
300000+ - 1500000	0,00%	0,00%	6,67%	0,00%	6,67%	40,00%	46,67%
More than 1500000	7,14%	0,00%	0,00%	0,00%	7,14%	28,57%	57,14%

Table 4.8.5 When you do use Chrome how useful are they to you? Broken out by Gender of survey participant

Gender of survey participant	No Answer	Don't use this at all	Not very useful	Somewhat useful	Useful	Quite useful	Essential
Male	0,00%	20,00%	0,00%	0,00%	0,00%	40,00%	40,00%
Female	1,82%	10,91%	5,45%	1,82%	18,18%	23,64%	38,18%

Table 4.9.1 When you do use Google Books how useful are they to you?

	No Answer	Don't use this at all	Not very useful	Somewhat useful	Useful	Quite useful	Essential
Entire sample	1,67%	46,67%	3,33%	15,00%	16,67%	8,33%	8,33%

Table 4.9.2 When you do use Google Books how useful are they to you? Broken out by Population size of the area served

Population size of the area served	No Answer	Don't use this at all	Not very useful	Somewhat useful	Useful	Quite useful	Essential
Less than 2000	0,00%	85,71%	0,00%	7,14%	0,00%	7,14%	0,00%
2000 - 10000	0,00%	46,67%	6,67%	6,67%	20,00%	13,33%	6,67%
10000+ - 45000	6,67%	20,00%	6,67%	20,00%	40,00%	0,00%	6,67%
More than 45000	0,00%	37,50%	0,00%	25,00%	6,25%	12,50%	18,75%

Table 4.9.3 When you do use Google Books how useful are they to you? Broken out by Age range of survey participant

Age range of survey participant	No Answer	Don't use this at all	Not very useful	Somewhat useful	Useful	Quite useful	Essential
Under 30	0,00%	0,00%	0,00%	0,00%	0,00%	33,33%	66,67%
30-39	14,29%	14,29%	0,00%	28,57%	14,29%	28,57%	0,00%
40-49	0,00%	33,33%	8,33%	0,00%	25,00%	8,33%	25,00%
50-59	0,00%	60,00%	0,00%	20,00%	16,00%	4,00%	0,00%
60-69	0,00%	50,00%	10,00%	20,00%	20,00%	0,00%	0,00%
70 or Over	0,00%	100,00%	0,00%	0,00%	0,00%	0,00%	0,00%

Table 4.9.4 When you do use Google Books how useful are they to you? Broken out by Library's annual budget, $

Library's annual budget, $	No Answer	Don't use this at all	Not very useful	Somewhat useful	Useful	Quite useful	Essential
Less than 50000	0,00%	73,33%	0,00%	6,67%	13,33%	6,67%	0,00%
50000 - 300000	6,25%	50,00%	0,00%	12,50%	18,75%	6,25%	6,25%
300000+ - 1500000	0,00%	26,67%	13,33%	33,33%	13,33%	6,67%	6,67%
More than 1500000	0,00%	35,71%	0,00%	7,14%	21,43%	14,29%	21,43%

Table 4.9.5 When you do use Google Books how useful are they to you? Broken out by Gender of survey participant

Gender of survey participant	No Answer	Don't use this at all	Not very useful	Somewhat useful	Useful	Quite useful	Essential
Male	20,00%	40,00%	0,00%	20,00%	20,00%	0,00%	0,00%
Female	0,00%	47,27%	3,64%	14,55%	16,36%	9,09%	9,09%

Table 4.10.1 When you do use Google Scholar how useful are they to you?

	Don't use this at all	Not very useful	Somewhat useful	Useful	Quite useful	Essential
Entire sample	65,00%	3,33%	5,00%	11,67%	5,00%	10,00%

Table 4.10.2 When you do use Google Scholar how useful are they to you? Broken out by Population size of the area served

Population size of the area served	Don't use this at all	Not very useful	Somewhat useful	Useful	Quite useful	Essential
Less than 2000	92,86%	0,00%	7,14%	0,00%	0,00%	0,00%
2000 - 10000	66,67%	6,67%	6,67%	13,33%	0,00%	6,67%
10000+ - 45000	46,67%	6,67%	6,67%	13,33%	13,33%	13,33%
More than 45000	56,25%	0,00%	0,00%	18,75%	6,25%	18,75%

Table 4.10.3 When you do use Google Scholar how useful are they to you? Broken out by Age range of survey participant

Age range of survey participant	Don't use this at all	Not very useful	Somewhat useful	Useful	Quite useful	Essential
Under 30	0,00%	0,00%	0,00%	33,33%	0,00%	66,67%
30-39	57,14%	0,00%	0,00%	0,00%	28,57%	14,29%
40-49	50,00%	8,33%	0,00%	16,67%	0,00%	25,00%
50-59	76,00%	0,00%	8,00%	12,00%	4,00%	0,00%
60-69	70,00%	10,00%	10,00%	10,00%	0,00%	0,00%
70 or Over	100,00%	0,00%	0,00%	0,00%	0,00%	0,00%

Table 4.10.4 When you do use Google Scholar how useful are they to you? Broken out by Library's annual budget, $

Library's annual budget, $	Don't use this at all	Not very useful	Somewhat useful	Useful	Quite useful	Essential
Less than 50000	100,00%	0,00%	0,00%	0,00%	0,00%	0,00%
50000 - 300000	56,25%	0,00%	18,75%	6,25%	12,50%	6,25%
300000+ - 1500000	46,67%	13,33%	0,00%	26,67%	6,67%	6,67%
More than 1500000	57,14%	0,00%	0,00%	14,29%	0,00%	28,57%

Table 4.10.5 When you do use Google Scholar how useful are they to you? Broken out by Gender of survey participant

Gender of survey participant	Don't use this at all	Not very useful	Somewhat useful	Useful	Quite useful	Essential
Male	40,00%	0,00%	0,00%	0,00%	40,00%	20,00%
Female	67,27%	3,64%	5,45%	12,73%	1,82%	9,09%

Table 4.11.1 When you do use Google Scholar My Citations how useful are they to you?

	No Answer	Don't use this at all	Not very useful	Somewhat useful	Useful	Quite useful	Essential
Entire sample	1,67%	75,00%	3,33%	6,67%	8,33%	3,33%	1,67%

Table 4.11.2 When you do use Google Scholar My Citations how useful are they to you? Broken out by Population size of the area served

Population size of the area served	No Answer	Don't use this at all	Not very useful	Somewhat useful	Useful	Quite useful	Essential
Less than 2000	0,00%	100,00%	0,00%	0,00%	0,00%	0,00%	0,00%
2000 - 10000	0,00%	66,67%	13,33%	0,00%	13,33%	0,00%	6,67%
10000+ - 45000	0,00%	60,00%	0,00%	13,33%	20,00%	6,67%	0,00%
More than 45000	6,25%	75,00%	0,00%	12,50%	0,00%	6,25%	0,00%

Table 4.11.3 When you do use Google Scholar My Citations how useful are they to you? Broken out by Age range of survey participant

Age range of survey participant	No Answer	Don't use this at all	Not very useful	Somewhat useful	Useful	Quite useful	Essential
Under 30	0,00%	33,33%	0,00%	33,33%	33,33%	0,00%	0,00%
30-39	0,00%	71,43%	0,00%	0,00%	14,29%	14,29%	0,00%
40-49	0,00%	58,33%	8,33%	0,00%	16,67%	8,33%	8,33%
50-59	4,00%	84,00%	4,00%	4,00%	4,00%	0,00%	0,00%
60-69	0,00%	80,00%	0,00%	20,00%	0,00%	0,00%	0,00%
70 or Over	0,00%	100,00%	0,00%	0,00%	0,00%	0,00%	0,00%

Table 4.11.4 When you do use Google Scholar My Citations how useful are they to you? Broken out by Library's annual budget, $

Library's annual budget, $	No Answer	Don't use this at all	Not very useful	Somewhat useful	Useful	Quite useful	Essential
Less than 50000	0,00%	100,00%	0,00%	0,00%	0,00%	0,00%	0,00%
50000 - 300000	0,00%	68,75%	6,25%	6,25%	12,50%	0,00%	6,25%
300000+ - 1500000	6,67%	53,33%	6,67%	13,33%	20,00%	0,00%	0,00%
More than 1500000	0,00%	78,57%	0,00%	7,14%	0,00%	14,29%	0,00%

Table 4.11.5 When you do use Google Scholar My Citations how useful are they to you? Broken out by Gender of survey participant

Gender of survey participant	No Answer	Don't use this at all	Not very useful	Somewhat useful	Useful	Quite useful	Essential
Male	0,00%	60,00%	0,00%	0,00%	20,00%	20,00%	0,00%
Female	1,82%	76,36%	3,64%	7,27%	7,27%	1,82%	1,82%

Table 4.12.1 When you do use Google Translate how useful are they to you?

	Don't use this at all	Not very useful	Somewhat useful	Useful	Quite useful	Essential
Entire sample	33,33%	1,67%	18,33%	21,67%	16,67%	8,33%

Table 4.12.2 When you do use Google Translate how useful are they to you? Broken out by Population size of the area served

Population size of the area served	Don't use this at all	Not very useful	Somewhat useful	Useful	Quite useful	Essential
Less than 2000	50,00%	0,00%	35,71%	14,29%	0,00%	0,00%
2000 - 10000	33,33%	0,00%	13,33%	26,67%	20,00%	6,67%
10000+ - 45000	26,67%	0,00%	26,67%	13,33%	33,33%	0,00%
More than 45000	25,00%	6,25%	0,00%	31,25%	12,50%	25,00%

Table 4.12.3 When you do use Google Translate how useful are they to you? Broken out by Age range of survey participant

Age range of survey participant	Don't use this at all	Not very useful	Somewhat useful	Useful	Quite useful	Essential
Under 30	33,33%	0,00%	0,00%	0,00%	33,33%	33,33%
30-39	14,29%	0,00%	28,57%	14,29%	42,86%	0,00%
40-49	33,33%	0,00%	8,33%	25,00%	8,33%	25,00%
50-59	36,00%	4,00%	16,00%	28,00%	16,00%	0,00%
60-69	40,00%	0,00%	30,00%	10,00%	10,00%	10,00%
70 or Over	33,33%	0,00%	33,33%	33,33%	0,00%	0,00%

Table 4.12.4 When you do use Google Translate how useful are they to you? Broken out by Library's annual budget, $

Library's annual budget, $	Don't use this at all	Not very useful	Somewhat useful	Useful	Quite useful	Essential
Less than 50000	46,67%	0,00%	26,67%	26,67%	0,00%	0,00%
50000 - 300000	37,50%	0,00%	18,75%	18,75%	18,75%	6,25%
300000+ - 1500000	26,67%	6,67%	26,67%	20,00%	20,00%	0,00%
More than 1500000	21,43%	0,00%	0,00%	21,43%	28,57%	28,57%

Table 4.12.5 When you do use Google Translate how useful are they to you? Broken out by Gender of survey participant

Gender of survey participant	Don't use this at all	Not very useful	Somewhat useful	Useful	Quite useful	Essential
Male	20,00%	0,00%	0,00%	20,00%	60,00%	0,00%
Female	34,55%	1,82%	20,00%	21,82%	12,73%	9,09%

Table 4.13.1 When you do use Google Public Data Explorer how useful are they to you?

	No Answer	Don't use this at all	Not very useful	Somewhat useful	Useful	Quite useful	Essential
Entire sample	1,67%	73,33%	6,67%	8,33%	10,00%	0,00%	0,00%

Table 4.13.2 When you do use Google Public Data Explorer how useful are they to you? Broken out by Population size of the area served

Population size of the area served	No Answer	Don't use this at all	Not very useful	Somewhat useful	Useful	Quite useful	Essential
Less than 2000	0,00%	100,00%	0,00%	0,00%	0,00%	0,00%	0,00%
2000 - 10000	0,00%	66,67%	13,33%	0,00%	20,00%	0,00%	0,00%
10000+ - 45000	0,00%	73,33%	6,67%	20,00%	0,00%	0,00%	0,00%
More than 45000	6,25%	56,25%	6,25%	12,50%	18,75%	0,00%	0,00%

Table 4.13.3 When you do use Google Public Data Explorer how useful are they to you? Broken out by Age range of survey participant

Age range of survey participant	No Answer	Don't use this at all	Not very useful	Somewhat useful	Useful	Quite useful	Essential
Under 30	0,00%	66,67%	33,33%	0,00%	0,00%	0,00%	0,00%
30-39	0,00%	71,43%	0,00%	14,29%	14,29%	0,00%	0,00%
40-49	0,00%	50,00%	8,33%	0,00%	41,67%	0,00%	0,00%
50-59	4,00%	84,00%	4,00%	8,00%	0,00%	0,00%	0,00%
60-69	0,00%	70,00%	10,00%	20,00%	0,00%	0,00%	0,00%
70 or Over	0,00%	100,00%	0,00%	0,00%	0,00%	0,00%	0,00%

Table 4.13.4 When you do use Google Public Data Explorer how useful are they to you? Broken out by Library's annual budget, $

Library's annual budget, $	No Answer	Don't use this at all	Not very useful	Somewhat useful	Useful	Quite useful	Essential
Less than 50000	0,00%	100,00%	0,00%	0,00%	0,00%	0,00%	0,00%
50000 - 300000	0,00%	75,00%	6,25%	6,25%	12,50%	0,00%	0,00%
300000+ - 1500000	6,67%	53,33%	13,33%	13,33%	13,33%	0,00%	0,00%
More than 1500000	0,00%	64,29%	7,14%	14,29%	14,29%	0,00%	0,00%

Table 4.13.5 When you do use Google Public Data Explorer how useful are they to you? Broken out by Gender of survey participant

Gender of survey participant	No Answer	Don't use this at all	Not very useful	Somewhat useful	Useful	Quite useful	Essential
Male	0,00%	60,00%	0,00%	20,00%	20,00%	0,00%	0,00%
Female	1,82%	74,55%	7,27%	7,27%	9,09%	0,00%	0,00%

Table 4.14.1 When you do use Google Drive how useful are they to you?

	Don't use this at all	Not very useful	Somewhat useful	Useful	Quite useful	Essential
Entire sample	38,33%	10,00%	6,67%	6,67%	13,33%	25,00%

Table 4.14.2 When you do use Google Drive how useful are they to you? Broken out by Population size of the area served

Population size of the area served	Don't use this at all	Not very useful	Somewhat useful	Useful	Quite useful	Essential
Less than 2000	57,14%	7,14%	7,14%	0,00%	21,43%	7,14%
2000 - 10000	26,67%	20,00%	6,67%	13,33%	6,67%	26,67%
10000+ - 45000	40,00%	13,33%	6,67%	0,00%	6,67%	33,33%
More than 45000	31,25%	0,00%	6,25%	12,50%	18,75%	31,25%

Table 4.14.3 When you do use Google Drive how useful are they to you? Broken out by Age range of survey participant

Age range of survey participant	Don't use this at all	Not very useful	Somewhat useful	Useful	Quite useful	Essential
Under 30	33,33%	0,00%	0,00%	0,00%	0,00%	66,67%
30-39	0,00%	0,00%	0,00%	0,00%	42,86%	57,14%
40-49	25,00%	0,00%	0,00%	16,67%	16,67%	41,67%
50-59	48,00%	8,00%	16,00%	8,00%	4,00%	16,00%

60-69	50,00%	30,00%	0,00%	0,00%	20,00%	0,00%
70 or Over	66,67%	33,33%	0,00%	0,00%	0,00%	0,00%

Table 4.14.4 When you do use Google Drive how useful are they to you? Broken out by Library's annual budget, $

Library's annual budget, $	Don't use this at all	Not very useful	Somewhat useful	Useful	Quite useful	Essential
Less than 50000	53,33%	13,33%	6,67%	0,00%	13,33%	13,33%
50000 - 300000	50,00%	18,75%	0,00%	12,50%	6,25%	12,50%
300000+ - 1500000	13,33%	6,67%	20,00%	6,67%	13,33%	40,00%
More than 1500000	35,71%	0,00%	0,00%	7,14%	21,43%	35,71%

Table 4.14.5 When you do use Google Drive how useful are they to you? Broken out by Gender of survey participant

Gender of survey participant	Don't use this at all	Not very useful	Somewhat useful	Useful	Quite useful	Essential
Male	40,00%	0,00%	0,00%	0,00%	20,00%	40,00%
Female	38,18%	10,91%	7,27%	7,27%	12,73%	23,64%

Table 4.15.1 When you do use Google Earth how useful are they to you?

	Don't use this at all	Not very useful	Somewhat useful	Useful	Quite useful	Essential
Entire sample	21,67%	5,00%	23,33%	30,00%	10,00%	10,00%

Table 4.15.2 When you do use Google Earth how useful are they to you? Broken out by Population size of the area served

Population size of the area served	Don't use this at all	Not very useful	Somewhat useful	Useful	Quite useful	Essential
Less than 2000	28,57%	7,14%	21,43%	35,71%	7,14%	0,00%
2000 - 10000	13,33%	6,67%	13,33%	46,67%	0,00%	20,00%
10000+ - 45000	13,33%	6,67%	33,33%	20,00%	20,00%	6,67%
More than 45000	31,25%	0,00%	25,00%	18,75%	12,50%	12,50%

Table 4.15.3 When you do use Google Earth how useful are they to you? Broken out by Age range of survey participant

Age range of survey participant	Don't use this at all	Not very useful	Somewhat useful	Useful	Quite useful	Essential
Under 30	66,67%	0,00%	0,00%	0,00%	0,00%	33,33%
30-39	0,00%	0,00%	28,57%	14,29%	42,86%	14,29%
40-49	8,33%	8,33%	33,33%	41,67%	0,00%	8,33%
50-59	28,00%	0,00%	20,00%	36,00%	8,00%	8,00%
60-69	20,00%	20,00%	30,00%	10,00%	10,00%	10,00%
70 or Over	33,33%	0,00%	0,00%	66,67%	0,00%	0,00%

Table 4.15.4 When you do use Google Earth how useful are they to you? Broken out by Library's annual budget, $

Library's annual budget, $	Don't use this at all	Not very useful	Somewhat useful	Useful	Quite useful	Essential
Less than 50000	33,33%	6,67%	13,33%	40,00%	6,67%	0,00%
50000 - 300000	18,75%	0,00%	25,00%	37,50%	6,25%	12,50%
300000+ - 1500000	13,33%	13,33%	26,67%	20,00%	13,33%	13,33%
More than 1500000	21,43%	0,00%	28,57%	21,43%	14,29%	14,29%

Table 4.15.5 When you do use Google Earth how useful are they to you? Broken out by Gender of survey participant

Gender of survey participant	Don't use this at all	Not very useful	Somewhat useful	Useful	Quite useful	Essential
Male	0,00%	0,00%	60,00%	0,00%	40,00%	0,00%
Female	23,64%	5,45%	20,00%	32,73%	7,27%	10,91%

Table 4.16.1 When you do use Google Sky how useful are they to you?

	No Answer	Don't use this at all	Not very useful	Somewhat useful	Useful	Quite useful	Essential
Entire sample	6,67%	63,33%	3,33%	11,67%	6,67%	6,67%	1,67%

Table 4.16.2 When you do use Google Sky how useful are they to you? Broken out by Population size of the area served

Population size of the area served	No Answer	Don't use this at all	Not very useful	Somewhat useful	Useful	Quite useful	Essential
Less than 2000	7,14%	78,57%	0,00%	7,14%	0,00%	7,14%	0,00%
2000 - 10000	6,67%	66,67%	6,67%	0,00%	20,00%	0,00%	0,00%
10000+ - 45000	6,67%	46,67%	6,67%	26,67%	0,00%	13,33%	0,00%
More than 45000	6,25%	62,50%	0,00%	12,50%	6,25%	6,25%	6,25%

Table 4.16.3 When you do use Google Sky how useful are they to you? Broken out by Age range of survey participant

Age range of survey participant	No Answer	Don't use this at all	Not very useful	Somewhat useful	Useful	Quite useful	Essential
Under 30	0,00%	66,67%	0,00%	0,00%	0,00%	33,33%	0,00%
30-39	0,00%	42,86%	0,00%	14,29%	0,00%	42,86%	0,00%
40-49	8,33%	58,33%	8,33%	8,33%	16,67%	0,00%	0,00%
50-59	8,00%	72,00%	0,00%	12,00%	8,00%	0,00%	0,00%
60-69	10,00%	60,00%	10,00%	10,00%	0,00%	0,00%	10,00%
70 or Over	0,00%	66,67%	0,00%	33,33%	0,00%	0,00%	0,00%

Table 4.16.4 When you do use Google Sky how useful are they to you? Broken out by Library's annual budget, $

Library's annual budget, $	No Answer	Don't use this at all	Not very useful	Somewhat useful	Useful	Quite useful	Essential
Less than 50000	6,67%	80,00%	0,00%	6,67%	0,00%	6,67%	0,00%
50000 - 300000	6,25%	68,75%	0,00%	6,25%	12,50%	6,25%	0,00%
300000+ - 1500000	6,67%	40,00%	13,33%	20,00%	6,67%	13,33%	0,00%
More than 1500000	7,14%	64,29%	0,00%	14,29%	7,14%	0,00%	7,14%

Table 4.16.5 When you do use Google Sky how useful are they to you? Broken out by Gender of survey participant

Gender of survey participant	No Answer	Don't use this at all	Not very useful	Somewhat useful	Useful	Quite useful	Essential
Male	0,00%	40,00%	0,00%	20,00%	0,00%	40,00%	0,00%
Female	7,27%	65,45%	3,64%	10,91%	7,27%	3,64%	1,82%

Table 4.17.1 When you do use Google+ how useful are they to you?

	No Answer	Don't use this at all	Not very useful	Somewhat useful	Useful	Quite useful	Essential
Entire sample	1,67%	56,67%	10,00%	16,67%	5,00%	6,67%	3,33%

Table 4.17.2 When you do use Google+ how useful are they to you? Broken out by Population size of the area served

Population size of the area served	No Answer	Don't use this at all	Not very useful	Somewhat useful	Useful	Quite useful	Essential
Less than 2000	0,00%	78,57%	7,14%	7,14%	0,00%	7,14%	0,00%
2000 - 10000	6,67%	53,33%	0,00%	20,00%	13,33%	0,00%	6,67%
10000+ - 45000	0,00%	46,67%	26,67%	6,67%	6,67%	6,67%	6,67%
More than 45000	0,00%	50,00%	6,25%	31,25%	0,00%	12,50%	0,00%

Table 4.17.3 When you do use Google+ how useful are they to you? Broken out by Age range of survey participant

Age range of survey participant	No Answer	Don't use this at all	Not very useful	Somewhat useful	Useful	Quite useful	Essential
Under 30	0,00%	100,00%	0,00%	0,00%	0,00%	0,00%	0,00%
30-39	0,00%	28,57%	14,29%	28,57%	0,00%	28,57%	0,00%
40-49	0,00%	58,33%	0,00%	25,00%	16,67%	0,00%	0,00%
50-59	0,00%	56,00%	12,00%	20,00%	0,00%	4,00%	8,00%
60-69	0,00%	60,00%	20,00%	0,00%	10,00%	10,00%	0,00%
70 or Over	33,33%	66,67%	0,00%	0,00%	0,00%	0,00%	0,00%

Table 4.17.4 When you do use Google+ how useful are they to you? Broken out by Library's annual budget, $

Library's annual budget, $	No Answer	Don't use this at all	Not very useful	Somewhat useful	Useful	Quite useful	Essential
Less than 50000	6,67%	73,33%	0,00%	6,67%	0,00%	13,33%	0,00%
50000 - 300000	0,00%	43,75%	12,50%	18,75%	12,50%	6,25%	6,25%
300000+ - 1500000	0,00%	60,00%	20,00%	13,33%	0,00%	0,00%	6,67%
More than 1500000	0,00%	50,00%	7,14%	28,57%	7,14%	7,14%	0,00%

Table 4.17.5 When you do use Google+ how useful are they to you? Broken out by Gender of survey participant

Gender of survey participant	No Answer	Don't use this at all	Not very useful	Somewhat useful	Useful	Quite useful	Essential
Male	0,00%	60,00%	20,00%	0,00%	0,00%	20,00%	0,00%
Female	1,82%	56,36%	9,09%	18,18%	5,45%	5,45%	3,64%

Table 4.18.1 When you do use Google Hangouts how useful are they to you?

	No Answer	Don't use this at all	Not very useful	Somewhat useful	Useful	Quite useful	Essential
Entire sample	5,00%	51,67%	3,33%	16,67%	10,00%	8,33%	5,00%

Table 4.18.2 When you do use Google Hangouts how useful are they to you? Broken out by Population size of the area served

Population size of the area served	No Answer	Don't use this at all	Not very useful	Somewhat useful	Useful	Quite useful	Essential
Less than 2000	7,14%	71,43%	0,00%	14,29%	0,00%	0,00%	7,14%
2000 - 10000	6,67%	46,67%	0,00%	6,67%	26,67%	0,00%	13,33%
10000+ - 45000	0,00%	46,67%	13,33%	13,33%	6,67%	20,00%	0,00%
More than 45000	6,25%	43,75%	0,00%	31,25%	6,25%	12,50%	0,00%

Table 4.18.3 When you do use Google Hangouts how useful are they to you? Broken out by Age range of survey participant

Age range of survey participant	No Answer	Don't use this at all	Not very useful	Somewhat useful	Useful	Quite useful	Essential
Under 30	0,00%	100,00%	0,00%	0,00%	0,00%	0,00%	0,00%
30-39	0,00%	14,29%	0,00%	14,29%	0,00%	42,86%	28,57%
40-49	0,00%	41,67%	0,00%	25,00%	33,33%	0,00%	0,00%
50-59	4,00%	60,00%	4,00%	16,00%	8,00%	4,00%	4,00%
60-69	0,00%	60,00%	10,00%	20,00%	0,00%	10,00%	0,00%
70 or Over	66,67%	33,33%	0,00%	0,00%	0,00%	0,00%	0,00%

Table 4.18.4 When you do use Google Hangouts how useful are they to you? Broken out by Library's annual budget, $

Library's annual budget, $	No Answer	Don't use this at all	Not very useful	Somewhat useful	Useful	Quite useful	Essential
Less than 50000	13,33%	80,00%	0,00%	6,67%	0,00%	0,00%	0,00%
50000 - 300000	0,00%	43,75%	6,25%	12,50%	18,75%	6,25%	12,50%
300000+ - 1500000	6,67%	46,67%	6,67%	13,33%	13,33%	6,67%	6,67%
More than 1500000	0,00%	35,71%	0,00%	35,71%	7,14%	21,43%	0,00%

Table 4.18.5 When you do use Google Hangouts how useful are they to you? Broken out by Gender of survey participant

Gender of survey participant	No Answer	Don't use this at all	Not very useful	Somewhat useful	Useful	Quite useful	Essential
Male	0,00%	40,00%	0,00%	0,00%	0,00%	60,00%	0,00%
Female	5,45%	52,73%	3,64%	18,18%	10,91%	3,64%	5,45%

Table 4.19.1 When you do use Gmail how useful are they to you?

	No Answer	Don't use this at all	Not very useful	Somewhat useful	Useful	Quite useful	Essential
Entire sample	1,67%	5,00%	0,00%	13,33%	10,00%	13,33%	56,67%

Table 4.19.2 When you do use Gmail how useful are they to you? Broken out by Population size of the area served

Population size of the area served	No Answer	Don't use this at all	Not very useful	Somewhat useful	Useful	Quite useful	Essential
Less than 2000	0,00%	7,14%	0,00%	21,43%	14,29%	35,71%	21,43%
2000 - 10000	0,00%	0,00%	0,00%	6,67%	6,67%	6,67%	80,00%
10000+ - 45000	6,67%	13,33%	0,00%	13,33%	13,33%	0,00%	53,33%
More than 45000	0,00%	0,00%	0,00%	12,50%	6,25%	12,50%	68,75%

Table 4.19.3 When you do use Gmail how useful are they to you? Broken out by Age range of survey participant

Age range of survey participant	No Answer	Don't use this at all	Not very useful	Somewhat useful	Useful	Quite useful	Essential
Under 30	0,00%	0,00%	0,00%	0,00%	0,00%	0,00%	100,00%
30-39	0,00%	0,00%	0,00%	0,00%	0,00%	42,86%	57,14%
40-49	0,00%	0,00%	0,00%	8,33%	16,67%	0,00%	75,00%
50-59	0,00%	0,00%	0,00%	16,00%	4,00%	12,00%	68,00%
60-69	10,00%	20,00%	0,00%	30,00%	10,00%	20,00%	10,00%
70 or Over	0,00%	33,33%	0,00%	0,00%	66,67%	0,00%	0,00%

Table 4.19.4 When you do use Gmail how useful are they to you? Broken out by Library's annual budget, $

Library's annual budget, $	No Answer	Don't use this at all	Not very useful	Somewhat useful	Useful	Quite useful	Essential
Less than 50000	0,00%	6,67%	0,00%	6,67%	26,67%	40,00%	20,00%
50000 - 300000	0,00%	6,25%	0,00%	25,00%	0,00%	0,00%	68,75%
300000+ - 1500000	0,00%	6,67%	0,00%	13,33%	6,67%	6,67%	66,67%
More than 1500000	7,14%	0,00%	0,00%	7,14%	7,14%	7,14%	71,43%

Table 4.19.5 When you do use Gmail how useful are they to you? Broken out by Gender of survey participant

Gender of survey participant	No Answer	Don't use this at all	Not very useful	Somewhat useful	Useful	Quite useful	Essential
Male	0,00%	20,00%	0,00%	0,00%	0,00%	20,00%	60,00%
Female	1,82%	3,64%	0,00%	14,55%	10,91%	12,73%	56,36%

Table 4.20.1 When you do use Google Bookmarks how useful are they to you?

	No Answer	Don't use this at all	Not very useful	Somewhat useful	Useful	Quite useful	Essential
Entire sample	3,33%	56,67%	0,00%	16,67%	8,33%	3,33%	11,67%

Table 4.20.2 When you do use Google Bookmarks how useful are they to you? Broken out by Population size of the area served

Population size of the area served	No Answer	Don't use this at all	Not very useful	Somewhat useful	Useful	Quite useful	Essential
Less than 2000	0,00%	85,71%	0,00%	14,29%	0,00%	0,00%	0,00%
2000 - 10000	0,00%	53,33%	0,00%	0,00%	20,00%	0,00%	26,67%
10000+ - 45000	0,00%	53,33%	0,00%	13,33%	6,67%	6,67%	20,00%
More than 45000	12,50%	37,50%	0,00%	37,50%	6,25%	6,25%	0,00%

Table 4.20.3 When you do use Google Bookmarks how useful are they to you? Broken out by Age range of survey participant

Age range of survey participant	No Answer	Don't use this at all	Not very useful	Somewhat useful	Useful	Quite useful	Essential
Under 30	0,00%	33,33%	0,00%	33,33%	0,00%	0,00%	33,33%
30-39	0,00%	28,57%	0,00%	28,57%	14,29%	14,29%	14,29%
40-49	0,00%	50,00%	0,00%	8,33%	33,33%	0,00%	8,33%
50-59	8,00%	56,00%	0,00%	16,00%	0,00%	4,00%	16,00%
60-69	0,00%	80,00%	0,00%	20,00%	0,00%	0,00%	0,00%
70 or Over	0,00%	100,00%	0,00%	0,00%	0,00%	0,00%	0,00%

Table 4.20.4 When you do use Google Bookmarks how useful are they to you? Broken out by Library's annual budget, $

Library's annual budget, $	No Answer	Don't use this at all	Not very useful	Somewhat useful	Useful	Quite useful	Essential
Less than 50000	6,67%	86,67%	0,00%	6,67%	0,00%	0,00%	0,00%
50000 - 300000	0,00%	50,00%	0,00%	18,75%	6,25%	6,25%	18,75%
300000+ - 1500000	6,67%	40,00%	0,00%	13,33%	13,33%	0,00%	26,67%
More than 1500000	0,00%	50,00%	0,00%	28,57%	14,29%	7,14%	0,00%

Table 4.20.5 When you do use Google Bookmarks how useful are they to you? Broken out by Gender of survey participant

Gender of survey participant	No Answer	Don't use this at all	Not very useful	Somewhat useful	Useful	Quite useful	Essential
Male	0,00%	40,00%	0,00%	20,00%	20,00%	20,00%	0,00%
Female	3,64%	58,18%	0,00%	16,36%	7,27%	1,82%	12,73%

Table 4.21.1 When you do use Google Patent Search how useful are they to you?

	No Answer	Don't use this at all	Not very useful	Somewhat useful	Useful	Quite useful	Essential
Entire sample	1,67%	80,00%	0,00%	8,33%	6,67%	3,33%	0,00%

Table 4.21.2 When you do use Google Patent Search how useful are they to you? Broken out by Population size of the area served

Population size of the area served	No Answer	Don't use this at all	Not very useful	Somewhat useful	Useful	Quite useful	Essential
Less than 2000	0,00%	100,00%	0,00%	0,00%	0,00%	0,00%	0,00%
2000 - 10000	0,00%	73,33%	0,00%	13,33%	13,33%	0,00%	0,00%
10000+ - 45000	0,00%	80,00%	0,00%	6,67%	6,67%	6,67%	0,00%
More than 45000	6,25%	68,75%	0,00%	12,50%	6,25%	6,25%	0,00%

Table 4.21.3 When you do use Google Patent Search how useful are they to you? Broken out by Age range of survey participant

Age range of survey participant	No Answer	Don't use this at all	Not very useful	Somewhat useful	Useful	Quite useful	Essential
Under 30	0,00%	100,00%	0,00%	0,00%	0,00%	0,00%	0,00%
30-39	0,00%	57,14%	0,00%	0,00%	14,29%	28,57%	0,00%
40-49	0,00%	58,33%	0,00%	16,67%	25,00%	0,00%	0,00%
50-59	4,00%	88,00%	0,00%	8,00%	0,00%	0,00%	0,00%
60-69	0,00%	90,00%	0,00%	10,00%	0,00%	0,00%	0,00%
70 or Over	0,00%	100,00%	0,00%	0,00%	0,00%	0,00%	0,00%

Table 4.21.4 When you do use Google Patent Search how useful are they to you? Broken out by Library's annual budget, $

Library's annual budget, $	No Answer	Don't use this at all	Not very useful	Somewhat useful	Useful	Quite useful	Essential
Less than 50000	0,00%	100,00%	0,00%	0,00%	0,00%	0,00%	0,00%
50000 - 300000	0,00%	68,75%	0,00%	18,75%	6,25%	6,25%	0,00%
300000+ - 1500000	6,67%	73,33%	0,00%	6,67%	6,67%	6,67%	0,00%
More than 1500000	0,00%	78,57%	0,00%	7,14%	14,29%	0,00%	0,00%

Table 4.21.5 When you do use Google Patent Search how useful are they to you? Broken out by Gender of survey participant

Gender of survey participant	No Answer	Don't use this at all	Not very useful	Somewhat useful	Useful	Quite useful	Essential
Male	0,00%	40,00%	0,00%	0,00%	20,00%	40,00%	0,00%
Female	1,82%	83,64%	0,00%	9,09%	5,45%	0,00%	0,00%

Table 4.22.1 When you do use Google Forms how useful are they to you?

	No Answer	Don't use this at all	Not very useful	Somewhat useful	Useful	Quite useful	Essential
Entire sample	1,67%	58,33%	6,67%	5,00%	13,33%	10,00%	5,00%

Table 4.22.2 When you do use Google Forms how useful are they to you? Broken out by Population size of the area served

Population size of the area served	No Answer	Don't use this at all	Not very useful	Somewhat useful	Useful	Quite useful	Essential
Less than 2000	0,00%	85,71%	0,00%	0,00%	7,14%	0,00%	7,14%
2000 - 10000	0,00%	53,33%	13,33%	0,00%	6,67%	13,33%	13,33%
10000+ - 45000	0,00%	53,33%	13,33%	0,00%	20,00%	13,33%	0,00%
More than 45000	6,25%	43,75%	0,00%	18,75%	18,75%	12,50%	0,00%

Table 4.22.3 When you do use Google Forms how useful are they to you? Broken out by Age range of survey participant

Age range of survey participant	No Answer	Don't use this at all	Not very useful	Somewhat useful	Useful	Quite useful	Essential
Under 30	0,00%	100,00%	0,00%	0,00%	0,00%	0,00%	0,00%
30-39	0,00%	28,57%	0,00%	0,00%	0,00%	57,14%	14,29%
40-49	0,00%	33,33%	8,33%	8,33%	33,33%	8,33%	8,33%
50-59	4,00%	68,00%	8,00%	4,00%	12,00%	0,00%	4,00%
60-69	0,00%	60,00%	10,00%	10,00%	10,00%	10,00%	0,00%
70 or Over	0,00%	100,00%	0,00%	0,00%	0,00%	0,00%	0,00%

Table 4.22.4 When you do use Google Forms how useful are they to you? Broken out by Library's annual budget, $

Library's annual budget, $	No Answer	Don't use this at all	Not very useful	Somewhat useful	Useful	Quite useful	Essential
Less than 50000	0,00%	80,00%	0,00%	0,00%	13,33%	0,00%	6,67%
50000 - 300000	0,00%	62,50%	12,50%	0,00%	6,25%	18,75%	0,00%
300000+ - 1500000	6,67%	40,00%	13,33%	6,67%	13,33%	6,67%	13,33%

More than 1500000	0,00%	50,00%	0,00%	14,29%	21,43%	14,29%	0,00%

Table 4.22.5 When you do use Google Forms how useful are they to you? Broken out by Gender of survey participant

Gender of survey participant	No Answer	Don't use this at all	Not very useful	Somewhat useful	Useful	Quite useful	Essential
Male	0,00%	40,00%	0,00%	0,00%	0,00%	60,00%	0,00%
Female	1,82%	60,00%	7,27%	5,45%	14,55%	5,45%	5,45%

Table 4.23.1 When you do use Google Slides how useful are they to you?

	No Answer	Don't use this at all	Not very useful	Somewhat useful	Useful	Quite useful	Essential
Entire sample	3,33%	71,67%	3,33%	10,00%	6,67%	3,33%	1,67%

Table 4.23.2 When you do use Google Slides how useful are they to you? Broken out by Population size of the area served

Population size of the area served	No Answer	Don't use this at all	Not very useful	Somewhat useful	Useful	Quite useful	Essential
Less than 2000	0,00%	100,00%	0,00%	0,00%	0,00%	0,00%	0,00%
2000 - 10000	0,00%	60,00%	13,33%	13,33%	13,33%	0,00%	0,00%
10000+ - 45000	0,00%	73,33%	0,00%	13,33%	6,67%	6,67%	0,00%
More than 45000	12,50%	56,25%	0,00%	12,50%	6,25%	6,25%	6,25%

Table 4.23.3 When you do use Google Slides how useful are they to you? Broken out by Age range of survey participant

Age range of survey participant	No Answer	Don't use this at all	Not very useful	Somewhat useful	Useful	Quite useful	Essential
Under 30	0,00%	66,67%	0,00%	0,00%	0,00%	0,00%	33,33%
30-39	0,00%	42,86%	0,00%	0,00%	28,57%	28,57%	0,00%
40-49	0,00%	50,00%	8,33%	25,00%	16,67%	0,00%	0,00%
50-59	4,00%	84,00%	4,00%	8,00%	0,00%	0,00%	0,00%
60-69	10,00%	80,00%	0,00%	10,00%	0,00%	0,00%	0,00%
70 or Over	0,00%	100,00%	0,00%	0,00%	0,00%	0,00%	0,00%

Table 4.23.4 When you do use Google Slides how useful are they to you? Broken out by Library's annual budget, $

Library's annual budget, $	No Answer	Don't use this at all	Not very useful	Somewhat useful	Useful	Quite useful	Essential
Less than 50000	0,00%	93,33%	0,00%	6,67%	0,00%	0,00%	0,00%
50000 - 300000	0,00%	62,50%	6,25%	12,50%	12,50%	6,25%	0,00%
300000+ - 1500000	6,67%	66,67%	6,67%	13,33%	0,00%	6,67%	0,00%
More than 1500000	7,14%	64,29%	0,00%	7,14%	14,29%	0,00%	7,14%

Table 4.23.5 When you do use Google Slides how useful are they to you? Broken out by Gender of survey participant

Gender of survey participant	No Answer	Don't use this at all	Not very useful	Somewhat useful	Useful	Quite useful	Essential
Male	0,00%	40,00%	0,00%	0,00%	20,00%	40,00%	0,00%
Female	3,64%	74,55%	3,64%	10,91%	5,45%	0,00%	1,82%

Table 4.24.1 When you do use Google Groups how useful are they to you?

	No Answer	Don't use this at all	Not very useful	Somewhat useful	Useful	Quite useful	Essential
Entire sample	1,67%	63,33%	5,00%	13,33%	11,67%	3,33%	1,67%

Table 4.24.2 When you do use Google Groups how useful are they to you? Broken out by Population size of the area served

Population size of the area served	No Answer	Don't use this at all	Not very useful	Somewhat useful	Useful	Quite useful	Essential
Less than 2000	0,00%	85,71%	0,00%	7,14%	7,14%	0,00%	0,00%
2000 - 10000	0,00%	53,33%	13,33%	13,33%	13,33%	0,00%	6,67%
10000+ - 45000	0,00%	66,67%	6,67%	6,67%	13,33%	6,67%	0,00%
More than 45000	6,25%	50,00%	0,00%	25,00%	12,50%	6,25%	0,00%

Table 4.24.3 When you do use Google Groups how useful are they to you? Broken out by Age range of survey participant

Age range of survey participant	No Answer	Don't use this at all	Not very useful	Somewhat useful	Useful	Quite useful	Essential
Under 30	0,00%	66,67%	0,00%	33,33%	0,00%	0,00%	0,00%
30-39	0,00%	28,57%	0,00%	0,00%	42,86%	28,57%	0,00%
40-49	0,00%	50,00%	8,33%	16,67%	16,67%	0,00%	8,33%
50-59	4,00%	72,00%	4,00%	16,00%	4,00%	0,00%	0,00%
60-69	0,00%	70,00%	10,00%	10,00%	10,00%	0,00%	0,00%
70 or Over	0,00%	100,00%	0,00%	0,00%	0,00%	0,00%	0,00%

Table 4.24.4 When you do use Google Groups how useful are they to you? Broken out by Library's annual budget, $

Library's annual budget, $	No Answer	Don't use this at all	Not very useful	Somewhat useful	Useful	Quite useful	Essential
Less than 50000	0,00%	93,33%	0,00%	0,00%	6,67%	0,00%	0,00%
50000 - 300000	0,00%	50,00%	12,50%	18,75%	12,50%	6,25%	0,00%
300000+ - 1500000	6,67%	60,00%	6,67%	13,33%	0,00%	6,67%	6,67%
More than 1500000	0,00%	50,00%	0,00%	21,43%	28,57%	0,00%	0,00%

Table 4.24.5 When you do use Google Groups how useful are they to you? Broken out by Gender of survey participant

Gender of survey participant	No Answer	Don't use this at all	Not very useful	Somewhat useful	Useful	Quite useful	Essential
Male	0,00%	40,00%	0,00%	0,00%	20,00%	40,00%	0,00%
Female	1,82%	65,45%	5,45%	14,55%	10,91%	0,00%	1,82%

Table 4.25.1 When you do use Google Analytics how useful are they to you?

	Don't use this at all	Not very useful	Somewhat useful	Useful	Quite useful	Essential
Entire sample	61,67%	3,33%	10,00%	8,33%	8,33%	8,33%

Table 4.25.2 When you do use Google Analytics how useful are they to you? Broken out by Population size of the area served

Population size of the area served	Don't use this at all	Not very useful	Somewhat useful	Useful	Quite useful	Essential
Less than 2000	85,71%	0,00%	0,00%	7,14%	7,14%	0,00%
2000 - 10000	60,00%	6,67%	13,33%	6,67%	6,67%	6,67%
10000+ - 45000	60,00%	6,67%	13,33%	6,67%	0,00%	13,33%
More than 45000	43,75%	0,00%	12,50%	12,50%	18,75%	12,50%

Table 4.25.3 When you do use Google Analytics how useful are they to you? Broken out by Age range of survey participant

Age range of survey participant	Don't use this at all	Not very useful	Somewhat useful	Useful	Quite useful	Essential
Under 30	100,00%	0,00%	0,00%	0,00%	0,00%	0,00%
30-39	42,86%	0,00%	0,00%	0,00%	28,57%	28,57%
40-49	25,00%	0,00%	8,33%	25,00%	16,67%	25,00%
50-59	72,00%	4,00%	12,00%	8,00%	4,00%	0,00%
60-69	70,00%	10,00%	20,00%	0,00%	0,00%	0,00%
70 or Over	100,00%	0,00%	0,00%	0,00%	0,00%	0,00%

Table 4.25.4 When you do use Google Analytics how useful are they to you? Broken out by Library's annual budget, $

Library's annual budget, $	Don't use this at all	Not very useful	Somewhat useful	Useful	Quite useful	Essential
Less than 50000	86,67%	0,00%	0,00%	6,67%	6,67%	0,00%
50000 - 300000	62,50%	12,50%	12,50%	6,25%	0,00%	6,25%
300000+ - 1500000	40,00%	0,00%	20,00%	13,33%	20,00%	6,67%
More than 1500000	57,14%	0,00%	7,14%	7,14%	7,14%	21,43%

Table 4.25.5 When you do use Google Analytics how useful are they to you? Broken out by Gender of survey participant

Gender of survey participant	Don't use this at all	Not very useful	Somewhat useful	Useful	Quite useful	Essential
Male	40,00%	0,00%	0,00%	0,00%	20,00%	40,00%
Female	63,64%	3,64%	10,91%	9,09%	7,27%	5,45%

Table 4.26.1 When you do use Blogger how useful are they to you?

	No Answer	Don't use this at all	Not very useful	Somewhat useful	Useful	Quite useful	Essential
Entire sample	1,67%	71,67%	6,67%	6,67%	5,00%	3,33%	5,00%

Table 4.26.2 When you do use Blogger how useful are they to you? Broken out by Population size of the area served

Population size of the area served	No Answer	Don't use this at all	Not very useful	Somewhat useful	Useful	Quite useful	Essential
Less than 2000	0,00%	92,86%	0,00%	0,00%	0,00%	7,14%	0,00%
2000 - 10000	0,00%	60,00%	13,33%	0,00%	13,33%	6,67%	6,67%
10000+ - 45000	0,00%	73,33%	13,33%	0,00%	6,67%	0,00%	6,67%
More than 45000	6,25%	62,50%	0,00%	25,00%	0,00%	0,00%	6,25%

Table 4.26.3 When you do use Blogger how useful are they to you? Broken out by Age range of survey participant

Age range of survey participant	No Answer	Don't use this at all	Not very useful	Somewhat useful	Useful	Quite useful	Essential
Under 30	0,00%	0,00%	0,00%	33,33%	0,00%	0,00%	66,67%
30-39	0,00%	57,14%	14,29%	0,00%	14,29%	14,29%	0,00%
40-49	0,00%	58,33%	0,00%	8,33%	16,67%	8,33%	8,33%
50-59	4,00%	84,00%	8,00%	4,00%	0,00%	0,00%	0,00%
60-69	0,00%	80,00%	10,00%	10,00%	0,00%	0,00%	0,00%
70 or Over	0,00%	100,00%	0,00%	0,00%	0,00%	0,00%	0,00%

Table 4.26.4 When you do use Blogger how useful are they to you? Broken out by Library's annual budget, $

Library's annual budget, $	No Answer	Don't use this at all	Not very useful	Somewhat useful	Useful	Quite useful	Essential
Less than 50000	0,00%	93,33%	0,00%	0,00%	0,00%	6,67%	0,00%
50000 - 300000	0,00%	62,50%	18,75%	0,00%	12,50%	0,00%	6,25%
300000+ - 1500000	6,67%	66,67%	0,00%	6,67%	6,67%	6,67%	6,67%
More than 1500000	0,00%	64,29%	7,14%	21,43%	0,00%	0,00%	7,14%

Table 4.26.5 When you do use Blogger how useful are they to you? Broken out by Gender of survey participant

Gender of survey participant	No Answer	Don't use this at all	Not very useful	Somewhat useful	Useful	Quite useful	Essential
Male	0,00%	80,00%	20,00%	0,00%	0,00%	0,00%	0,00%
Female	1,82%	70,91%	5,45%	7,27%	5,45%	3,64%	5,45%

Table 4.27.1 When you do use YouTube how useful are they to you?

	No Answer	Don't use this at all	Not very useful	Somewhat useful	Useful	Quite useful	Essential
Entire sample	1,67%	5,00%	6,67%	21,67%	25,00%	18,33%	21,67%

Table 4.27.2 When you do use YouTube how useful are they to you? Broken out by Population size of the area served

Population size of the area served	No Answer	Don't use this at all	Not very useful	Somewhat useful	Useful	Quite useful	Essential
Less than 2000	7,14%	7,14%	0,00%	28,57%	42,86%	14,29%	0,00%
2000 - 10000	0,00%	0,00%	20,00%	20,00%	20,00%	20,00%	20,00%
10000+ - 45000	0,00%	13,33%	0,00%	20,00%	20,00%	6,67%	40,00%
More than 45000	0,00%	0,00%	6,25%	18,75%	18,75%	31,25%	25,00%

Table 4.27.3 When you do use YouTube how useful are they to you? Broken out by Age range of survey participant

Age range of survey participant	No Answer	Don't use this at all	Not very useful	Somewhat useful	Useful	Quite useful	Essential
Under 30	0,00%	0,00%	0,00%	0,00%	0,00%	0,00%	100,00%
30-39	14,29%	0,00%	0,00%	28,57%	14,29%	14,29%	28,57%
40-49	0,00%	8,33%	8,33%	16,67%	33,33%	16,67%	16,67%
50-59	0,00%	4,00%	8,00%	16,00%	28,00%	24,00%	20,00%
60-69	0,00%	10,00%	0,00%	40,00%	20,00%	20,00%	10,00%
70 or Over	0,00%	0,00%	33,33%	33,33%	33,33%	0,00%	0,00%

Table 4.27.4 When you do use YouTube how useful are they to you? Broken out by Library's annual budget, $

Library's annual budget, $	No Answer	Don't use this at all	Not very useful	Somewhat useful	Useful	Quite useful	Essential
Less than 50000	6,67%	0,00%	6,67%	33,33%	33,33%	20,00%	0,00%
50000 - 300000	0,00%	12,50%	6,25%	12,50%	31,25%	12,50%	25,00%
300000+ - 1500000	0,00%	0,00%	13,33%	33,33%	26,67%	6,67%	20,00%
More than 1500000	0,00%	7,14%	0,00%	7,14%	7,14%	35,71%	42,86%

Table 4.27.5 When you do use YouTube how useful are they to you? Broken out by Gender of survey participant

Gender of survey participant	No Answer	Don't use this at all	Not very useful	Somewhat useful	Useful	Quite useful	Essential
Male	0,00%	20,00%	0,00%	40,00%	0,00%	0,00%	40,00%
Female	1,82%	3,64%	7,27%	20,00%	27,27%	20,00%	20,00%

For those Google features that you labeled "Quite Useful" or "Essential" what were these features and what do you use them for?

Less than 2000

1) n/a
2) Gmail and Chrome. I regularly use Gmail for my personal email (but not my library email). Chrome is generally my browser of choice. I use it to look up information, for ordering of supplies, to connect me to pretty much anything I want to get to on the internet.
3) Google drive: use it for all our financial forms, and documents, calendar :staff schedule and social events
4) Chrome, Google Calendar, Google Hangouts, and Gmail. Chrome is the browser used by all computers, public and staff, in the library. Google calendar is used to schedule our public meeting space. I am available on hangouts all day every day to keep in touch with people offsite. Gmail is the system used by library staff to send and receive e-mail.
5) Maps I use for directions, especially the street view for places that I have never been to; Images are used frequently in our library for clipart; Gmail is useful because I have a tablet that utilizes Google; I use YouTube to access music and learn about new sounds.
6) I mainly use chrome as the browser. I like the way it's set up to show multiple websites
7) Chrome is my daily default browser at both home and work. I find the search engine the most helpful and least frustrating of all. At the library if a patron is having troubles with the computer, quite often the issue stems from using Internet Explorer. I always redirect them to Chrome which resolves the issue. I also use Firefox as that's the preferred browser for our circulation system. I use the map feature weekly for myself, patrons, co-workers, everyone. I love being able to switch back and forth to satellite to really see where I'm going.
8) NA
9) I use Google maps for directions and Google Calendar in the library so the staff is aware of what is going on.
10) Google maps is my GPS. gmail is my email

2000 - 10000

1) Maps - Traveling Images - Designing Bulletin Board & Cards Gmail - Library's & Personal, Don't Like Yahoo At All!
2) Daily personal and work use
3) Communicating and coordinating with other colleagues for the most part
4) Chrome-internet searches Gmail-email
5) YouTube - author visits; chrome - searches; maps - travel plans; images and photos - library related book jacket, clip art, etc.
6) Email, images, photos, directions -- These are all needed in my work.
7) Google Maps and Google earth are handy when traveling.
8) Communication, knowledge, learning and directions, of course!

9) Looking to see where patrons live.
10) browser
11) reference and social media
12) Google Notifications - helpful with what to expect next, Google Images - very helpful with decorating bulletin boards, Gmail - absolutely wonderful, Google Bookmarks - use it every day.

10000+ - 45000

1) Maps: Directions for patrons/offsite trainings, Advanced Search: specific searches/searches that can bring back a lot of varied results, Images: flyers/displays/signs, Photos: storing and transferring photos taken with phone at offsite events, Chrome: everything, Books: finding book/research, Scholar: historical/academic searches, Translate: to understand what a book is about when searching for Spanish materials to add to collection, Drive: sharing and storing files, Earth: finding trails for patrons, Gmail: all email communication, Bookmarks: saving and organizing important pages, Blogger: library staff memos, YouTube: library videos
2) I use Google Maps street view before a trip so I'm familiar with the streets and exits. Chrome loads faster when I'm in a hurry. Can't live without email, so Gmail is a must. You can learn to do anything on YouTube and watch Ellen. Google Translate does an amazing job of translation which is vital in my community. Google Scholar just saves time in searches.
3) print directions for patrons, find cc pictures, staff calendar, collaborate on docs
4) Directions, reminders, mapping out library and personal calendars, browsing, documents all library personnel edit or view, email
5) use for work
6) Marketing the library and finding creative commons images for displays.
7) Work calendar, search engine for all searches, all my photos are stored on Google
8) Google maps - directions and locating places; Google images - for images; Google calendar - to coordinate work & personal calendars
9) Pictures for flyers/color sheets/reports/etc. Maps-help patrons find directions/maps to training Translation for patrons/flyers, etc.
10) Use maps to reach homebound patrons. Photos to illustrate concepts and add ambiance to content. Translate for patrons or terms used in books. Google Groups not professionally but in personal life. Google Drive to access library shared info, YouTube to evaluate performers for programs. Chrome almost all the time.

More than 45000

1) Google Maps- I usually use this to see where things are when I travel. I prefer to look at a map and determine the best route rather than having GPS tell me where to go. This has proven to be very effective, and on one occasion I beat 4 other cars to the destination because I chose my route by looking at Google Maps while they all relied on GPS. Google Advanced Search, Images and Chrome -- I am a keyword searcher and use

these answer questions and find resources. Google Translate--I use this to convert English to French, for the most part. I have forgotten much of the French I learned in my youth, but now that my daughter is a 3rd year French student, I enjoy being able to say a few things to her in French. I just want to be sure I am saying what I think I am saying. Google Drive--This is a marvelous tool! Years ago, I moved all of our library's statistics onto spreadsheets in Google Docs and, eventually, they ended up in Drive. Drive allows us to collaborate on documents more easily, and the constant saving is fantastic. Gmail--I got started using Gmail ages ago for personal email, and I still like it. It is clean and simple. YouTube--I watch the occasional YouTube video, sometimes for entertainment, sometimes for education.

2) Finding specific information for clients and managing my information
3) There are too many to list them all. Most of the quite useful features I use are to find information for myself or for patrons. Google Drive, Photos, Hangouts, Gmail, Forms, Slides are for their respective tasks-- store files in an easy to share location, or communicate with others.
4) Advanced search because it narrows down what I'm looking for; Gmail, drive, calendar are all work related; YouTube and Images for visual help (and fun stuff); bookmarks to keep track of websites; and translate because I only read English.
5) Maps--Patrons ask for directions relatively frequently Advanced Search--I use it for just about every search, albeit in the background (e.g., I limit searches using the "site:", or the phrase search--all from the basic search box.) Gmail--my personal email program; for communication with colleagues outside my library system
6) All are often used during reference work or customers use them so we are called on to help with them.
7) Analytics for tracking web page use, Maps for patrons, Images for internal promotions, Chrome for general searches for info
8) check my Gmail & watch you tube videos, & use google to search for things online
9) Searchability of Google Books and the detail of Google Maps and Google Earth. I love the time slider in Google Earth. My life would not function without Gmail.
10) Maps, images, calendar, chrome, books, scholar, translate, drive, Gmail, slides, YouTube- all things I use for work and more often than their competitors.
11) Google Translate to communicate with our patrons who do not speak English. I have also used when traveling & in the airport very successfully to communicate with non-English speakers. Use Google maps almost every day to check directions. YouTube is great for finding directions on how to do things. Useful for myself and our library patrons. Google Earth and Sky are just fascinating to look at.
12) Google Maps for directions, Advanced Search for answering reference question, Photos and Images for research or to help a patron, You Tube for videos, Forms for interoffice; Hangouts for meetings; the others for work
13) Good web browser, very intuitive
14) We use Google for business

15) Chrome is my preferred browser. Gmail is my main email account.

Table 5 Approximately how much time in the past month have you personally spent (in hours or fractions thereof) using the following Google features in connection with your work? If you have not used the feature in the past month put in a zero.

Table 5.1.1 Approximately how much time in the past month have you personally spent (in hours or fractions thereof) using Google Maps in connection with your work? If you have not used the feature in the past month put in a zero.

	Mean	Median	Minimum	Maximum
Entire sample	4,63	1,00	0,00	100,00

Table 5.1.2 Approximately how much time in the past month have you personally spent (in hours or fractions thereof) using Google Maps in connection with your work? If you have not used the feature in the past month put in a zero. Broken out by Population size of the area served

Population size of the area served	Mean	Median	Minimum	Maximum
Less than 2000	1,13	0,75	0,00	5,00
2000 - 10000	4,09	1,00	0,00	24,00
10000+ - 45000	9,35	1,00	0,00	100,00
More than 45000	3,62	2,00	0,00	20,00

Table 5.1.3 Approximately how much time in the past month have you personally spent (in hours or fractions thereof) using Google Maps in connection with your work? If you have not used the feature in the past month put in a zero. Broken out by Age range of survey participant

Age range of survey participant	Mean	Median	Minimum	Maximum
Under 30	0,83	1,00	0,50	1,00
30-39	2,25	2,00	0,00	5,00
40-49	5,11	3,00	0,25	20,00
50-59	7,54	1,00	0,00	100,00
60-69	1,72	1,00	0,00	6,00
70 or Over	0,50	0,50	0,00	1,00

Table 5.1.4 Approximately how much time in the past month have you personally spent (in hours or fractions thereof) using Google Maps in connection with your work? If you have not used the feature in the past month put in a zero. Broken out by Library's annual budget, $

Library's annual budget, $	Mean	Median	Minimum	Maximum
Less than 50000	1,42	0,75	0,00	5,00
50000 - 300000	3,77	1,00	0,00	24,00
300000+ - 1500000	8,56	1,00	0,00	100,00
More than 1500000	4,13	2,00	0,25	20,00

Table 5.1.5 Approximately how much time in the past month have you personally spent (in hours or fractions thereof) using Google Maps in connection with your work? If you have not used the feature in the past month put in a zero. Broken out by Gender of survey participant

Gender of survey participant	Mean	Median	Minimum	Maximum
Male	2,38	2,25	0,00	5,00
Female	4,83	1,00	0,00	100,00

Table 5.2.1 Approximately how much time in the past month have you personally spent (in hours or fractions thereof) using Google Advanced Search in connection with your work? If you have not used the feature in the past month put in a zero.

	Mean	Median	Minimum	Maximum
Entire sample	4,58	0,00	0,00	100,00

Table 5.2.2 Approximately how much time in the past month have you personally spent (in hours or fractions thereof) using Google Advanced Search in connection with your work? If you have not used the feature in the past month put in a zero. Broken out by Population size of the area served

Population size of the area served	Mean	Median	Minimum	Maximum
Less than 2000	0,95	0,00	0,00	10,00
2000 - 10000	3,52	0,60	0,00	25,00
10000+ - 45000	8,13	0,25	0,00	100,00
More than 45000	4,92	1,00	0,00	30,00

Table 5.2.3 Approximately how much time in the past month have you personally spent (in hours or fractions thereof) using Google Advanced Search in connection with your work? If you have not used the feature in the past month put in a zero. Broken out by Age range of survey participant

Age range of survey participant	Mean	Median	Minimum	Maximum
Under 30	1,17	0,50	0,00	3,00
30-39	2,00	0,50	0,00	10,00
40-49	2,46	1,00	0,00	10,00
50-59	8,67	0,00	0,00	100,00
60-69	2,00	0,00	0,00	12,00
70 or Over	0,00	0,00	0,00	0,00

Table 5.2.4 Approximately how much time in the past month have you personally spent (in hours or fractions thereof) using Google Advanced Search in connection with your work? If you have not used the feature in the past month put in a zero. Broken out by Library's annual budget, $

Library's annual budget, $	Mean	Median	Minimum	Maximum
Less than 50000	3,64	0,00	0,00	30,00
50000 - 300000	2,71	0,25	0,00	25,00
300000+ - 1500000	8,84	1,00	0,00	100,00
More than 1500000	2,55	0,00	0,00	12,00

Table 5.2.5 Approximately how much time in the past month have you personally spent (in hours or fractions thereof) using Google Advanced Search in connection with your work? If you have not used the feature in the past month put in a zero. Broken out by Gender of survey participant

Gender of survey participant	Mean	Median	Minimum	Maximum
Male	0,80	1,00	0,00	2,00
Female	5,03	0,00	0,00	100,00

Table 5.3.1 Approximately how much time in the past month have you personally spent (in hours or fractions thereof) using Google Alerts in connection with your work? If you have not used the feature in the past month put in a zero.

	Mean	Median	Minimum	Maximum
Entire sample	2,43	0,00	0,00	100,00

Table 5.3.2 Approximately how much time in the past month have you personally spent (in hours or fractions thereof) using Google Alerts in connection with your work? If you have not used the feature in the past month put in a zero. Broken out by Population size of the area served

Population size of the area served	Mean	Median	Minimum	Maximum
Less than 2000	0,02	0,00	0,00	0,25
2000 - 10000	0,55	0,00	0,00	3,00
10000+ - 45000	8,04	0,00	0,00	100,00
More than 45000	0,13	0,00	0,00	1,00

Table 5.3.3 Approximately how much time in the past month have you personally spent (in hours or fractions thereof) using Google Alerts in connection with your work? If you have not used the feature in the past month put in a zero. Broken out by Age range of survey participant

Age range of survey participant	Mean	Median	Minimum	Maximum
Under 30	0,00	0,00	0,00	0,00
30-39	0,21	0,00	0,00	1,00
40-49	0,43	0,50	0,00	1,00
50-59	5,66	0,00	0,00	100,00
60-69	0,00	0,00	0,00	0,00
70 or Over	0,00	0,00	0,00	0,00

Table 5.3.4 Approximately how much time in the past month have you personally spent (in hours or fractions thereof) using Google Alerts in connection with your work? If you have not used the feature in the past month put in a zero. Broken out by Library's annual budget, $

Library's annual budget, $	Mean	Median	Minimum	Maximum
Less than 50000	0,02	0,00	0,00	0,25
50000 - 300000	0,25	0,00	0,00	3,00
300000+ - 1500000	8,31	0,50	0,00	100,00
More than 1500000	0,05	0,00	0,00	0,50

Table 5.3.5 Approximately how much time in the past month have you personally spent (in hours or fractions thereof) using Google Alerts in connection with your work? If you have not used the feature in the past month put in a zero. Broken out by Gender of survey participant

Gender of survey participant	Mean	Median	Minimum	Maximum
Male	0,20	0,00	0,00	1,00
Female	2,70	0,00	0,00	100,00

Table 5.4.1 Approximately how much time in the past month have you personally spent (in hours or fractions thereof) using Google Notifications in connection with your work? If you have not used the feature in the past month put in a zero.

	Mean	Median	Minimum	Maximum
Entire sample	2,41	0,00	0,00	100,00

Table 5.4.2 Approximately how much time in the past month have you personally spent (in hours or fractions thereof) using Google Notifications in connection with your work? If you have not used the feature in the past month put in a zero. Broken out by Population size of the area served

Population size of the area served	Mean	Median	Minimum	Maximum
Less than 2000	0,48	0,00	0,00	5,00
2000 - 10000	0,15	0,00	0,00	1,00
10000+ - 45000	8,02	0,00	0,00	100,00
More than 45000	0,00	0,00	0,00	0,00

Table 5.4.3 Approximately how much time in the past month have you personally spent (in hours or fractions thereof) using Google Notifications in connection with your work? If you have not used the feature in the past month put in a zero. Broken out by Age range of survey participant

Age range of survey participant	Mean	Median	Minimum	Maximum
Under 30	0,00	0,00	0,00	0,00
30-39	0,04	0,00	0,00	0,25
40-49	0,04	0,00	0,00	0,25
50-59	5,82	0,00	0,00	100,00
60-69	0,00	0,00	0,00	0,00
70 or Over	0,00	0,00	0,00	0,00

Table 5.4.4 Approximately how much time in the past month have you personally spent (in hours or fractions thereof) using Google Notifications in connection with your work? If you have not used the feature in the past month put in a zero. Broken out by Library's annual budget, $

Library's annual budget, $	Mean	Median	Minimum	Maximum
Less than 50000	0,02	0,00	0,00	0,25
50000 - 300000	0,50	0,00	0,00	5,00
300000+ - 1500000	8,06	0,00	0,00	100,00
More than 1500000	0,00	0,00	0,00	0,00

Table 5.4.5 Approximately how much time in the past month have you personally spent (in hours or fractions thereof) using Google Notifications in connection with your work? If you have not used the feature in the past month put in a zero. Broken out by Gender of survey participant

Gender of survey participant	Mean	Median	Minimum	Maximum
Male	0,00	0,00	0,00	0,00
Female	2,71	0,00	0,00	100,00

Table 5.5.1 Approximately how much time in the past month have you personally spent (in hours or fractions thereof) using Google Images in connection with your work? If you have not used the feature in the past month put in a zero.

	Mean	Median	Minimum	Maximum
Entire sample	6,21	1,00	0,00	100,00

Table 5.5.2 Approximately how much time in the past month have you personally spent (in hours or fractions thereof) using Google Images in connection with your work? If you have not used the feature in the past month put in a zero. Broken out by Population size of the area served

Population size of the area served	Mean	Median	Minimum	Maximum
Less than 2000	4,04	0,50	0,00	25,00
2000 - 10000	6,64	2,00	0,00	50,00
10000+ - 45000	11,62	2,00	0,00	100,00
More than 45000	2,46	1,00	0,00	10,00

Table 5.5.3 Approximately how much time in the past month have you personally spent (in hours or fractions thereof) using Google Images in connection with your work? If you have not used the feature in the past month put in a zero. Broken out by Age range of survey participant

Age range of survey participant	Mean	Median	Minimum	Maximum
Under 30	2,33	1,00	1,00	5,00
30-39	7,67	5,00	0,00	25,00
40-49	3,21	2,00	0,50	10,00
50-59	9,62	1,00	0,00	100,00
60-69	2,94	1,00	0,00	20,00
70 or Over	0,17	0,00	0,00	0,50

Table 5.5.4 Approximately how much time in the past month have you personally spent (in hours or fractions thereof) using Google Images in connection with your work? If you have not used the feature in the past month put in a zero. Broken out by Library's annual budget, $

Library's annual budget, $	Mean	Median	Minimum	Maximum
Less than 50000	6,04	1,00	0,00	25,00
50000 - 300000	6,15	1,00	0,00	50,00
300000+ - 1500000	9,62	2,00	0,00	100,00
More than 1500000	2,45	1,00	0,00	10,00

Table 5.5.5 Approximately how much time in the past month have you personally spent (in hours or fractions thereof) using Google Images in connection with your work? If you have not used the feature in the past month put in a zero. Broken out by Gender of survey participant

Gender of survey participant	Mean	Median	Minimum	Maximum
Male	3,20	1,00	0,00	10,00
Female	6,56	1,00	0,00	100,00

Table 5.6.1 Approximately how much time in the past month have you personally spent (in hours or fractions thereof) using Google Calendar in connection with your work? If you have not used the feature in the past month put in a zero.

	Mean	Median	Minimum	Maximum
Entire sample	6,82	0,50	0,00	100,00

Table 5.6.2 Approximately how much time in the past month have you personally spent (in hours or fractions thereof) using Google Calendar in connection with your work? If you have not used the feature in the past month put in a zero. Broken out by Population size of the area served

Population size of the area served	Mean	Median	Minimum	Maximum
Less than 2000	1,48	0,88	0,00	8,00
2000 - 10000	12,36	0,00	0,00	100,00
10000+ - 45000	10,69	1,00	0,00	100,00
More than 45000	3,19	0,00	0,00	25,00

Table 5.6.3 Approximately how much time in the past month have you personally spent (in hours or fractions thereof) using Google Calendar in connection with your work? If you have not used the feature in the past month put in a zero. Broken out by Age range of survey participant

Age range of survey participant	Mean	Median	Minimum	Maximum
Under 30	0,42	0,25	0,00	1,00
30-39	9,50	8,00	1,00	25,00
40-49	19,93	3,00	0,00	100,00
50-59	6,10	0,00	0,00	100,00
60-69	0,86	0,00	0,00	5,00
70 or Over	0,25	0,00	0,00	0,75

Table 5.6.4 Approximately how much time in the past month have you personally spent (in hours or fractions thereof) using Google Calendar in connection with your work? If you have not used the feature in the past month put in a zero. Broken out by Library's annual budget, $

Library's annual budget, $	Mean	Median	Minimum	Maximum
Less than 50000	1,40	0,38	0,00	8,00
50000 - 300000	1,23	0,00	0,00	10,00
300000+ - 1500000	21,25	4,00	0,00	100,00
More than 1500000	2,30	0,50	0,00	10,00

Table 5.6.5 Approximately how much time in the past month have you personally spent (in hours or fractions thereof) using Google Calendar in connection with your work? If you have not used the feature in the past month put in a zero. Broken out by Gender of survey participant

Gender of survey participant	Mean	Median	Minimum	Maximum
Male	8,60	8,00	0,00	25,00
Female	6,62	0,50	0,00	100,00

Table 5.7.1 Approximately how much time in the past month have you personally spent (in hours or fractions thereof) using Chrome in connection with your work? If you have not used the feature in the past month put in a zero.

	Mean	Median	Minimum	Maximum
Entire sample	33,82	10,00	0,00	160,00

Table 5.7.2 Approximately how much time in the past month have you personally spent (in hours or fractions thereof) using Chrome in connection with your work? If you have not used the feature in the past month put in a zero. Broken out by Population size of the area served

Population size of the area served	Mean	Median	Minimum	Maximum
Less than 2000	34,25	15,00	0,00	160,00
2000 - 10000	21,36	10,00	0,00	120,00
10000+ - 45000	35,25	10,00	0,00	130,00
More than 45000	42,54	10,00	0,00	140,00

Table 5.7.3 Approximately how much time in the past month have you personally spent (in hours or fractions thereof) using Chrome in connection with your work? If you have not used the feature in the past month put in a zero. Broken out by Age range of survey participant

Age range of survey participant	Mean	Median	Minimum	Maximum
Under 30	58,67	40,00	6,00	130,00
30-39	68,00	47,50	1,00	160,00
40-49	48,32	10,00	0,25	120,00
50-59	27,52	10,00	0,00	125,00
60-69	15,22	1,00	0,00	120,00
70 or Over	6,67	0,00	0,00	20,00

Table 5.7.4 Approximately how much time in the past month have you personally spent (in hours or fractions thereof) using Chrome in connection with your work? If you have not used the feature in the past month put in a zero. Broken out by Library's annual budget, $

Library's annual budget, $	Mean	Median	Minimum	Maximum
Less than 50000	20,08	10,00	0,00	125,00
50000 - 300000	25,54	10,00	0,00	120,00
300000+ - 1500000	52,85	10,00	1,00	160,00
More than 1500000	36,11	12,00	0,00	120,00

Table 5.7.5 Approximately how much time in the past month have you personally spent (in hours or fractions thereof) using Chrome in connection with your work? If you have not used the feature in the past month put in a zero. Broken out by Gender of survey participant

Gender of survey participant	Mean	Median	Minimum	Maximum
Male	44,40	12,00	0,00	140,00
Female	32,62	10,00	0,00	160,00

Table 5.8.1 Approximately how much time in the past month have you personally spent (in hours or fractions thereof) using Google Books in connection with your work? If you have not used the feature in the past month put in a zero.

	Mean	Median	Minimum	Maximum
Entire sample	0,81	0,00	0,00	10,00

Table 5.8.2 Approximately how much time in the past month have you personally spent (in hours or fractions thereof) using Google Books in connection with your work? If you have not used the feature in the past month put in a zero. Broken out by Population size of the area served

Population size of the area served	Mean	Median	Minimum	Maximum
Less than 2000	0,18	0,00	0,00	2,00
2000 - 10000	0,20	0,00	0,00	1,00
10000+ - 45000	0,82	0,10	0,00	5,00
More than 45000	1,88	0,00	0,00	10,00

Table 5.8.3 Approximately how much time in the past month have you personally spent (in hours or fractions thereof) using Google Books in connection with your work? If you have not used the feature in the past month put in a zero. Broken out by Age range of survey participant

Age range of survey participant	Mean	Median	Minimum	Maximum
Under 30	0,67	0,50	0,50	1,00
30-39	0,67	0,00	0,00	2,00
40-49	3,00	0,00	0,00	10,00
50-59	0,42	0,00	0,00	5,00
60-69	0,26	0,00	0,00	1,00
70 or Over	0,00	0,00	0,00	0,00

Table 5.8.4 Approximately how much time in the past month have you personally spent (in hours or fractions thereof) using Google Books in connection with your work? If you have not used the feature in the past month put in a zero. Broken out by Library's annual budget, $

Library's annual budget, $	Mean	Median	Minimum	Maximum
Less than 50000	0,18	0,00	0,00	2,00
50000 - 300000	0,50	0,00	0,00	2,00
300000+ - 1500000	0,50	0,00	0,00	5,00
More than 1500000	2,26	0,30	0,00	10,00

Table 5.8.5 Approximately how much time in the past month have you personally spent (in hours or fractions thereof) using Google Books in connection with your work? If you have not used the feature in the past month put in a zero. Broken out by Gender of survey participant

Gender of survey participant	Mean	Median	Minimum	Maximum
Male	0,40	0,00	0,00	2,00
Female	0,86	0,00	0,00	10,00

Table 5.9.1 Approximately how much time in the past month have you personally spent (in hours or fractions thereof) using Google Scholar in connection with your work? If you have not used the feature in the past month put in a zero.

	Mean	Median	Minimum	Maximum
Entire sample	0,46	0,00	0,00	10,00

Table 5.9.2 Approximately how much time in the past month have you personally spent (in hours or fractions thereof) using Google Scholar in connection with your work? If you have not used the feature in the past month put in a zero. Broken out by Population size of the area served

Population size of the area served	Mean	Median	Minimum	Maximum
Less than 2000	0,00	0,00	0,00	0,00
2000 - 10000	0,10	0,00	0,00	1,00
10000+ - 45000	0,54	0,00	0,00	2,00
More than 45000	1,08	0,00	0,00	10,00

Table 5.9.3 Approximately how much time in the past month have you personally spent (in hours or fractions thereof) using Google Scholar in connection with your work? If you have not used the feature in the past month put in a zero. Broken out by Age range of survey participant

Age range of survey participant	Mean	Median	Minimum	Maximum
Under 30	1,17	1,00	0,50	2,00
30-39	0,50	0,00	0,00	2,00
40-49	1,64	0,00	0,00	10,00
50-59	0,11	0,00	0,00	1,00
60-69	0,13	0,00	0,00	1,00
70 or Over	0,00	0,00	0,00	0,00

Table 5.9.4 Approximately how much time in the past month have you personally spent (in hours or fractions thereof) using Google Scholar in connection with your work? If you have not used the feature in the past month put in a zero. Broken out by Library's annual budget, $

Library's annual budget, $	Mean	Median	Minimum	Maximum
Less than 50000	0,00	0,00	0,00	0,00
50000 - 300000	0,33	0,00	0,00	1,00
300000+ - 1500000	0,15	0,00	0,00	1,00
More than 1500000	1,50	0,25	0,00	10,00

Table 5.9.5 Approximately how much time in the past month have you personally spent (in hours or fractions thereof) using Google Scholar in connection with your work? If you have not used the feature in the past month put in a zero. Broken out by Gender of survey participant

Gender of survey participant	Mean	Median	Minimum	Maximum
Male	0,60	0,00	0,00	2,00
Female	0,44	0,00	0,00	10,00

Table 5.10.1 Approximately how much time in the past month have you personally spent (in hours or fractions thereof) using Google Translate in connection with your work? If you have not used the feature in the past month put in a zero.

	Mean	Median	Minimum	Maximum
Entire sample	0,74	0,00	0,00	10,00

Table 5.10.2 Approximately how much time in the past month have you personally spent (in hours or fractions thereof) using Google Translate in connection with your work? If you have not used the feature in the past month put in a zero. Broken out by Population size of the area served

Population size of the area served	Mean	Median	Minimum	Maximum
Less than 2000	0,02	0,00	0,00	0,20
2000 - 10000	0,38	0,00	0,00	2,00
10000+ - 45000	1,23	1,00	0,00	5,00
More than 45000	1,17	0,25	0,00	10,00

Table 5.10.3 Approximately how much time in the past month have you personally spent (in hours or fractions thereof) using Google Translate in connection with your work? If you have not used the feature in the past month put in a zero. Broken out by Age range of survey participant

Age range of survey participant	Mean	Median	Minimum	Maximum
Under 30	0,67	1,00	0,00	1,00
30-39	0,83	0,00	0,00	3,00
40-49	2,00	0,50	0,00	10,00
50-59	0,39	0,00	0,00	5,00
60-69	0,69	0,01	0,00	3,00
70 or Over	0,00	0,00	0,00	0,00

Table 5.10.4 Approximately how much time in the past month have you personally spent (in hours or fractions thereof) using Google Translate in connection with your work? If you have not used the feature in the past month put in a zero. Broken out by Library's annual budget, $

Library's annual budget, $	Mean	Median	Minimum	Maximum
Less than 50000	0,27	0,00	0,00	3,00
50000 - 300000	0,60	0,00	0,00	3,00
300000+ - 1500000	0,64	0,00	0,00	5,00
More than 1500000	1,55	0,50	0,00	10,00

Table 5.10.5 Approximately how much time in the past month have you personally spent (in hours or fractions thereof) using Google Translate in connection with your work? If you have not used the feature in the past month put in a zero. Broken out by Gender of survey participant

Gender of survey participant	Mean	Median	Minimum	Maximum
Male	1,00	0,00	0,00	3,00
Female	0,71	0,00	0,00	10,00

Table 5.11.1 Approximately how much time in the past month have you personally spent (in hours or fractions thereof) using Google Public Data Explorer in connection with your work? If you have not used the feature in the past month put in a zero.

	Mean	Median	Minimum	Maximum
Entire sample	0,04	0,00	0,00	2,00

Table 5.11.2 Approximately how much time in the past month have you personally spent (in hours or fractions thereof) using Google Public Data Explorer in connection with your work? If you have not used the feature in the past month put in a zero. Broken out by Population size of the area served

Population size of the area served	Mean	Median	Minimum	Maximum
Less than 2000	0,00	0,00	0,00	0,00
2000 - 10000	0,00	0,00	0,00	0,00
10000+ - 45000	0,15	0,00	0,00	2,00
More than 45000	0,00	0,00	0,00	0,00

Table 5.11.3 Approximately how much time in the past month have you personally spent (in hours or fractions thereof) using Google Public Data Explorer in connection with your work? If you have not used the feature in the past month put in a zero. Broken out by Age range of survey participant

Age range of survey participant	Mean	Median	Minimum	Maximum
Under 30	0,00	0,00	0,00	0,00
30-39	0,00	0,00	0,00	0,00
40-49	0,00	0,00	0,00	0,00
50-59	0,11	0,00	0,00	2,00
60-69	0,00	0,00	0,00	0,00
70 or Over	0,00	0,00	0,00	0,00

Table 5.11.4 Approximately how much time in the past month have you personally spent (in hours or fractions thereof) using Google Public Data Explorer in connection with your work? If you have not used the feature in the past month put in a zero. Broken out by Library's annual budget, $

Library's annual budget, $	Mean	Median	Minimum	Maximum
Less than 50000	0,00	0,00	0,00	0,00
50000 - 300000	0,00	0,00	0,00	0,00
300000+ - 1500000	0,15	0,00	0,00	2,00
More than 1500000	0,00	0,00	0,00	0,00

Table 5.11.5 Approximately how much time in the past month have you personally spent (in hours or fractions thereof) using Google Public Data Explorer in connection with your work? If you have not used the feature in the past month put in a zero. Broken out by Gender of survey participant

Gender of survey participant	Mean	Median	Minimum	Maximum
Male	0,00	0,00	0,00	0,00
Female	0,05	0,00	0,00	2,00

Table 5.12.1 Approximately how much time in the past month have you personally spent (in hours or fractions thereof) using Google Drive in connection with your work? If you have not used the feature in the past month put in a zero.

	Mean	Median	Minimum	Maximum
Entire sample	5,57	0,00	0,00	100,00

Table 5.12.2 Approximately how much time in the past month have you personally spent (in hours or fractions thereof) using Google Drive in connection with your work? If you have not used the feature in the past month put in a zero. Broken out by Population size of the area served

Population size of the area served	Mean	Median	Minimum	Maximum
Less than 2000	4,18	0,00	0,00	25,00
2000 - 10000	4,33	0,15	0,00	30,00
10000+ - 45000	10,38	1,00	0,00	100,00
More than 45000	2,88	1,00	0,00	12,00

Table 5.12.3 Approximately how much time in the past month have you personally spent (in hours or fractions thereof) using Google Drive in connection with your work? If you have not used the feature in the past month put in a zero. Broken out by Age range of survey participant

Age range of survey participant	Mean	Median	Minimum	Maximum
Under 30	2,33	2,00	0,00	5,00
30-39	12,50	10,00	0,00	25,00
40-49	7,21	2,00	0,00	30,00
50-59	6,65	0,00	0,00	100,00
60-69	0,33	0,00	0,00	2,00
70 or Over	0,00	0,00	0,00	0,00

Table 5.12.4 Approximately how much time in the past month have you personally spent (in hours or fractions thereof) using Google Drive in connection with your work? If you have not used the feature in the past month put in a zero. Broken out by Library's annual budget, $

Library's annual budget, $	Mean	Median	Minimum	Maximum
Less than 50000	4,18	0,00	0,00	25,00
50000 - 300000	1,17	0,00	0,00	10,00
300000+ - 1500000	13,64	5,00	0,00	100,00
More than 1500000	2,23	0,50	0,00	10,00

Table 5.12.5 Approximately how much time in the past month have you personally spent (in hours or fractions thereof) using Google Drive in connection with your work? If you have not used the feature in the past month put in a zero. Broken out by Gender of survey participant

Gender of survey participant	Mean	Median	Minimum	Maximum
Male	6,00	10,00	0,00	10,00
Female	5,52	0,00	0,00	100,00

Table 5.13.1 Approximately how much time in the past month have you personally spent (in hours or fractions thereof) using Google Earth in connection with your work? If you have not used the feature in the past month put in a zero.

	Mean	Median	Minimum	Maximum
Entire sample	0,59	0,00	0,00	5,00

Table 5.13.2 Approximately how much time in the past month have you personally spent (in hours or fractions thereof) using Google Earth in connection with your work? If you have not used the feature in the past month put in a zero. Broken out by Population size of the area served

Population size of the area served	Mean	Median	Minimum	Maximum
Less than 2000	0,36	0,00	0,00	1,00
2000 - 10000	0,65	0,00	0,00	4,00
10000+ - 45000	0,62	0,00	0,00	3,00
More than 45000	0,69	0,00	0,00	5,00

Table 5.13.3 Approximately how much time in the past month have you personally spent (in hours or fractions thereof) using Google Earth in connection with your work? If you have not used the feature in the past month put in a zero. Broken out by Age range of survey participant

Age range of survey participant	Mean	Median	Minimum	Maximum
Under 30	0,17	0,00	0,00	0,50
30-39	0,33	0,00	0,00	1,00
40-49	1,07	0,00	0,00	5,00
50-59	0,53	0,00	0,00	4,00
60-69	0,72	0,50	0,00	2,00
70 or Over	0,33	0,00	0,00	1,00

Table 5.13.4 Approximately how much time in the past month have you personally spent (in hours or fractions thereof) using Google Earth in connection with your work? If you have not used the feature in the past month put in a zero. Broken out by Library's annual budget, $

Library's annual budget, $	Mean	Median	Minimum	Maximum
Less than 50000	0,36	0,00	0,00	1,00
50000 - 300000	1,00	0,00	0,00	4,00
300000+ - 1500000	0,27	0,00	0,00	1,00
More than 1500000	0,73	0,00	0,00	5,00

Table 5.13.5 Approximately how much time in the past month have you personally spent (in hours or fractions thereof) using Google Earth in connection with your work? If you have not used the feature in the past month put in a zero. Broken out by Gender of survey participant

Gender of survey participant	Mean	Median	Minimum	Maximum
Male	0,40	0,00	0,00	2,00
Female	0,61	0,00	0,00	5,00

Table 5.14.1 Approximately how much time in the past month have you personally spent (in hours or fractions thereof) using Google Sky in connection with your work? If you have not used the feature in the past month put in a zero.

	Mean	Median	Minimum	Maximum
Entire sample	0,01	0,00	0,00	0,50

Table 5.14.2 Approximately how much time in the past month have you personally spent (in hours or fractions thereof) using Google Sky in connection with your work? If you have not used the feature in the past month put in a zero. Broken out by Population size of the area served

Population size of the area served	Mean	Median	Minimum	Maximum
Less than 2000	0,00	0,00	0,00	0,00
2000 - 10000	0,00	0,00	0,00	0,00
10000+ - 45000	0,00	0,00	0,00	0,00
More than 45000	0,04	0,00	0,00	0,50

Table 5.14.3 Approximately how much time in the past month have you personally spent (in hours or fractions thereof) using Google Sky in connection with your work? If you have not used the feature in the past month put in a zero. Broken out by Age range of survey participant

Age range of survey participant	Mean	Median	Minimum	Maximum
Under 30	0,00	0,00	0,00	0,00
30-39	0,00	0,00	0,00	0,00
40-49	0,00	0,00	0,00	0,00
50-59	0,00	0,00	0,00	0,00
60-69	0,06	0,00	0,00	0,50
70 or Over	0,00	0,00	0,00	0,00

Table 5.14.4 Approximately how much time in the past month have you personally spent (in hours or fractions thereof) using Google Sky in connection with your work? If you have not used the feature in the past month put in a zero. Broken out by Library's annual budget, $

Library's annual budget, $	Mean	Median	Minimum	Maximum
Less than 50000	0,00	0,00	0,00	0,00
50000 - 300000	0,00	0,00	0,00	0,00
300000+ - 1500000	0,00	0,00	0,00	0,00
More than 1500000	0,05	0,00	0,00	0,50

Table 5.14.5 Approximately how much time in the past month have you personally spent (in hours or fractions thereof) using Google Sky in connection with your work? If you have not used the feature in the past month put in a zero. Broken out by Gender of survey participant

Gender of survey participant	Mean	Median	Minimum	Maximum
Male	0,00	0,00	0,00	0,00
Female	0,01	0,00	0,00	0,50

Table 5.15.1 Approximately how much time in the past month have you personally spent (in hours or fractions thereof) using Google+ in connection with your work? If you have not used the feature in the past month put in a zero.

	Mean	Median	Minimum	Maximum
Entire sample	1,13	0,00	0,00	30,00

Table 5.15.2 Approximately how much time in the past month have you personally spent (in hours or fractions thereof) using Google+ in connection with your work? If you have not used the feature in the past month put in a zero. Broken out by Population size of the area served

Population size of the area served	Mean	Median	Minimum	Maximum
Less than 2000	0,00	0,00	0,00	0,00
2000 - 10000	0,64	0,00	0,00	6,00
10000+ - 45000	1,23	0,00	0,00	10,00
More than 45000	2,50	0,00	0,00	30,00

Table 5.15.3 Approximately how much time in the past month have you personally spent (in hours or fractions thereof) using Google+ in connection with your work? If you have not used the feature in the past month put in a zero. Broken out by Age range of survey participant

Age range of survey participant	Mean	Median	Minimum	Maximum
Under 30	0,00	0,00	0,00	0,00
30-39	1,67	0,00	0,00	10,00
40-49	0,14	0,00	0,00	1,00
50-59	2,05	0,00	0,00	30,00
60-69	0,13	0,00	0,00	1,00
70 or Over	0,00	0,00	0,00	0,00

Table 5.15.4 Approximately how much time in the past month have you personally spent (in hours or fractions thereof) using Google+ in connection with your work? If you have not used the feature in the past month put in a zero. Broken out by Library's annual budget, $

Library's annual budget, $	Mean	Median	Minimum	Maximum
Less than 50000	2,73	0,00	0,00	30,00
50000 - 300000	1,38	0,00	0,00	10,00
300000+ - 1500000	0,38	0,00	0,00	4,00
More than 1500000	0,00	0,00	0,00	0,00

Table 5.15.5 Approximately how much time in the past month have you personally spent (in hours or fractions thereof) using Google+ in connection with your work? If you have not used the feature in the past month put in a zero. Broken out by Gender of survey participant

Gender of survey participant	Mean	Median	Minimum	Maximum
Male	2,00	0,00	0,00	10,00
Female	1,02	0,00	0,00	30,00

Table 5.16.1 Approximately how much time in the past month have you personally spent (in hours or fractions thereof) using Google Hangouts in connection with your work? If you have not used the feature in the past month put in a zero.

	Mean	Median	Minimum	Maximum
Entire sample	3,57	0,00	0,00	160,00

Table 5.16.2 Approximately how much time in the past month have you personally spent (in hours or fractions thereof) using Google Hangouts in connection with your work? If you have not used the feature in the past month put in a zero. Broken out by Population size of the area served

Population size of the area served	Mean	Median	Minimum	Maximum
Less than 2000	14,55	0,00	0,00	160,00
2000 - 10000	0,55	0,00	0,00	5,00
10000+ - 45000	0,19	0,00	0,00	2,00
More than 45000	0,23	0,00	0,00	1,00

Table 5.16.3 Approximately how much time in the past month have you personally spent (in hours or fractions thereof) using Google Hangouts in connection with your work? If you have not used the feature in the past month put in a zero. Broken out by Age range of survey participant

Age range of survey participant	Mean	Median	Minimum	Maximum
Under 30	0,00	0,00	0,00	0,00
30-39	27,17	0,50	0,00	160,00
40-49	0,21	0,00	0,00	1,00
50-59	0,25	0,00	0,00	5,00
60-69	0,22	0,00	0,00	1,00
70 or Over	0,00	0,00	0,00	0,00

Table 5.16.4 Approximately how much time in the past month have you personally spent (in hours or fractions thereof) using Google Hangouts in connection with your work? If you have not used the feature in the past month put in a zero. Broken out by Library's annual budget, $

Library's annual budget, $	Mean	Median	Minimum	Maximum
Less than 50000	0,00	0,00	0,00	0,00
50000 - 300000	0,38	0,00	0,00	5,00
300000+ - 1500000	12,50	0,00	0,00	160,00
More than 1500000	0,36	0,00	0,00	2,00

Table 5.16.5 Approximately how much time in the past month have you personally spent (in hours or fractions thereof) using Google Hangouts in connection with your work? If you have not used the feature in the past month put in a zero. Broken out by Gender of survey participant

Gender of survey participant	Mean	Median	Minimum	Maximum
Male	0,60	0,00	0,00	2,00
Female	3,92	0,00	0,00	160,00

Table 5.17.1 Approximately how much time in the past month have you personally spent (in hours or fractions thereof) using Gmail in connection with your work? If you have not used the feature in the past month put in a zero.

	Mean	Median	Minimum	Maximum
Entire sample	30,27	5,50	0,00	200,00

Table 5.17.2 Approximately how much time in the past month have you personally spent (in hours or fractions thereof) using Gmail in connection with your work? If you have not used the feature in the past month put in a zero. Broken out by Population size of the area served

Population size of the area served	Mean	Median	Minimum	Maximum
Less than 2000	18,00	1,00	0,00	160,00
2000 - 10000	44,05	6,00	0,00	200,00
10000+ - 45000	34,35	8,00	0,00	130,00
More than 45000	24,92	12,00	0,00	100,00

Table 5.17.3 Approximately how much time in the past month have you personally spent (in hours or fractions thereof) using Gmail in connection with your work? If you have not used the feature in the past month put in a zero. Broken out by Age range of survey participant

Age range of survey participant	Mean	Median	Minimum	Maximum
Under 30	90,00	100,00	40,00	130,00
30-39	36,33	14,00	0,00	160,00
40-49	68,43	40,00	0,00	200,00
50-59	15,77	2,25	0,00	100,00
60-69	18,17	3,00	0,00	120,00
70 or Over	2,33	2,00	1,00	4,00

Table 5.17.4 Approximately how much time in the past month have you personally spent (in hours or fractions thereof) using Gmail in connection with your work? If you have not used the feature in the past month put in a zero. Broken out by Library's annual budget, $

Library's annual budget, $	Mean	Median	Minimum	Maximum
Less than 50000	8,32	3,00	0,00	30,00
50000 - 300000	20,27	2,00	0,00	120,00
300000+ - 1500000	54,38	30,00	0,00	200,00
More than 1500000	35,55	12,00	0,00	120,00

Table 5.17.5 Approximately how much time in the past month have you personally spent (in hours or fractions thereof) using Gmail in connection with your work? If you have not used the feature in the past month put in a zero. Broken out by Gender of survey participant

Gender of survey participant	Mean	Median	Minimum	Maximum
Male	7,60	8,00	0,00	20,00
Female	32,91	5,00	0,00	200,00

Table 5.18.1 Approximately how much time in the past month have you personally spent (in hours or fractions thereof) using Google Bookmarks in connection with your work? If you have not used the feature in the past month put in a zero.

	Mean	Median	Minimum	Maximum
Entire sample	0,99	0,00	0,00	20,00

Table 5.18.2 Approximately how much time in the past month have you personally spent (in hours or fractions thereof) using Google Bookmarks in connection with your work? If you have not used the feature in the past month put in a zero. Broken out by Population size of the area served

Population size of the area served	Mean	Median	Minimum	Maximum
Less than 2000	0,64	0,00	0,00	5,00
2000 - 10000	0,24	0,00	0,00	2,00
10000+ - 45000	2,69	0,00	0,00	20,00
More than 45000	0,08	0,00	0,00	0,50

Table 5.18.3 Approximately how much time in the past month have you personally spent (in hours or fractions thereof) using Google Bookmarks in connection with your work? If you have not used the feature in the past month put in a zero. Broken out by Age range of survey participant

Age range of survey participant	Mean	Median	Minimum	Maximum
Under 30	6,67	0,00	0,00	20,00
30-39	0,17	0,00	0,00	1,00
40-49	0,29	0,00	0,00	2,00
50-59	1,15	0,00	0,00	10,00
60-69	0,06	0,00	0,00	0,50
70 or Over	0,00	0,00	0,00	0,00

Table 5.18.4 Approximately how much time in the past month have you personally spent (in hours or fractions thereof) using Google Bookmarks in connection with your work? If you have not used the feature in the past month put in a zero. Broken out by Library's annual budget, $

Library's annual budget, $	Mean	Median	Minimum	Maximum
Less than 50000	0,18	0,00	0,00	1,00
50000 - 300000	0,42	0,00	0,00	5,00
300000+ - 1500000	2,88	0,00	0,00	20,00
More than 1500000	0,10	0,00	0,00	0,50

Table 5.18.5 Approximately how much time in the past month have you personally spent (in hours or fractions thereof) using Google Bookmarks in connection with your work? If you have not used the feature in the past month put in a zero. Broken out by Gender of survey participant

Gender of survey participant	Mean	Median	Minimum	Maximum
Male	0,00	0,00	0,00	0,00
Female	1,11	0,00	0,00	20,00

Table 5.19.1 Approximately how much time in the past month have you personally spent (in hours or fractions thereof) using Google Patent Search in connection with your work? If you have not used the feature in the past month put in a zero.

	Mean	Median	Minimum	Maximum
Entire sample	0,00	0,00	0,00	0,00

Table 5.19.2 Approximately how much time in the past month have you personally spent (in hours or fractions thereof) using Google Patent Search in connection with your work? If you have not used the feature in the past month put in a zero. Broken out by Population size of the area served

Population size of the area served	Mean	Median	Minimum	Maximum
Less than 2000	0,00	0,00	0,00	0,00
2000 - 10000	0,00	0,00	0,00	0,00
10000+ - 45000	0,00	0,00	0,00	0,00
More than 45000	0,00	0,00	0,00	0,00

Table 5.19.3 Approximately how much time in the past month have you personally spent (in hours or fractions thereof) using Google Patent Search in connection with your work? If you have not used the feature in the past month put in a zero. Broken out by Age range of survey participant

Age range of survey participant	Mean	Median	Minimum	Maximum
Under 30	0,00	0,00	0,00	0,00
30-39	0,00	0,00	0,00	0,00
40-49	0,00	0,00	0,00	0,00
50-59	0,00	0,00	0,00	0,00
60-69	0,00	0,00	0,00	0,00
70 or Over	0,00	0,00	0,00	0,00

Table 5.19.4 Approximately how much time in the past month have you personally spent (in hours or fractions thereof) using Google Patent Search in connection with your work? If you have not used the feature in the past month put in a zero. Broken out by Library's annual budget, $

Library's annual budget, $	Mean	Median	Minimum	Maximum
Less than 50000	0,00	0,00	0,00	0,00
50000 - 300000	0,00	0,00	0,00	0,00
300000+ - 1500000	0,00	0,00	0,00	0,00
More than 1500000	0,00	0,00	0,00	0,00

Table 5.19.5 Approximately how much time in the past month have you personally spent (in hours or fractions thereof) using Google Patent Search in connection with your work? If you have not used the feature in the past month put in a zero. Broken out by Gender of survey participant

Gender of survey participant	Mean	Median	Minimum	Maximum
Male	0,00	0,00	0,00	0,00
Female	0,00	0,00	0,00	0,00

Table 5.20.1 Approximately how much time in the past month have you personally spent (in hours or fractions thereof) using Google Forms in connection with your work? If you have not used the feature in the past month put in a zero.

	Mean	Median	Minimum	Maximum
Entire sample	0,50	0,00	0,00	10,00

Table 5.20.2 Approximately how much time in the past month have you personally spent (in hours or fractions thereof) using Google Forms in connection with your work? If you have not used the feature in the past month put in a zero. Broken out by Population size of the area served

Population size of the area served	Mean	Median	Minimum	Maximum
Less than 2000	0,05	0,00	0,00	0,50
2000 - 10000	0,62	0,00	0,00	4,00
10000+ - 45000	0,77	0,00	0,00	10,00
More than 45000	0,54	0,00	0,00	3,00

Table 5.20.3 Approximately how much time in the past month have you personally spent (in hours or fractions thereof) using Google Forms in connection with your work? If you have not used the feature in the past month put in a zero. Broken out by Age range of survey participant

Age range of survey participant	Mean	Median	Minimum	Maximum
Under 30	0,33	0,00	0,00	1,00
30-39	0,50	0,00	0,00	3,00
40-49	0,86	0,00	0,00	4,00
50-59	0,04	0,00	0,00	0,50
60-69	1,44	0,00	0,00	10,00
70 or Over	0,00	0,00	0,00	0,00

Table 5.20.4 Approximately how much time in the past month have you personally spent (in hours or fractions thereof) using Google Forms in connection with your work? If you have not used the feature in the past month put in a zero. Broken out by Library's annual budget, $

Library's annual budget, $	Mean	Median	Minimum	Maximum
Less than 50000	0,95	0,00	0,00	10,00
50000 - 300000	0,08	0,00	0,00	1,00
300000+ - 1500000	0,63	0,00	0,00	4,00
More than 1500000	0,36	0,00	0,00	2,00

Table 5.20.5 Approximately how much time in the past month have you personally spent (in hours or fractions thereof) using Google Forms in connection with your work? If you have not used the feature in the past month put in a zero. Broken out by Gender of survey participant

Gender of survey participant	Mean	Median	Minimum	Maximum
Male	0,60	0,00	0,00	3,00
Female	0,49	0,00	0,00	10,00

Table 5.21.1 Approximately how much time in the past month have you personally spent (in hours or fractions thereof) using Google Slides in connection with your work? If you have not used the feature in the past month put in a zero.

	Mean	Median	Minimum	Maximum
Entire sample	0,07	0,00	0,00	1,00

Table 5.21.2 Approximately how much time in the past month have you personally spent (in hours or fractions thereof) using Google Slides in connection with your work? If you have not used the feature in the past month put in a zero. Broken out by Population size of the area served

Population size of the area served	Mean	Median	Minimum	Maximum
Less than 2000	0,00	0,00	0,00	0,00
2000 - 10000	0,00	0,00	0,00	0,00
10000+ - 45000	0,10	0,00	0,00	1,00
More than 45000	0,17	0,00	0,00	1,00

Table 5.21.3 Approximately how much time in the past month have you personally spent (in hours or fractions thereof) using Google Slides in connection with your work? If you have not used the feature in the past month put in a zero. Broken out by Age range of survey participant

Age range of survey participant	Mean	Median	Minimum	Maximum
Under 30	0,33	0,00	0,00	1,00
30-39	0,00	0,00	0,00	0,00
40-49	0,00	0,00	0,00	0,00
50-59	0,02	0,00	0,00	0,30
60-69	0,25	0,00	0,00	1,00
70 or Over	0,00	0,00	0,00	0,00

Table 5.21.4 Approximately how much time in the past month have you personally spent (in hours or fractions thereof) using Google Slides in connection with your work? If you have not used the feature in the past month put in a zero. Broken out by Library's annual budget, $

Library's annual budget, $	Mean	Median	Minimum	Maximum
Less than 50000	0,00	0,00	0,00	0,00
50000 - 300000	0,08	0,00	0,00	1,00
300000+ - 1500000	0,02	0,00	0,00	0,30
More than 1500000	0,20	0,00	0,00	1,00

Table 5.21.5 Approximately how much time in the past month have you personally spent (in hours or fractions thereof) using Google Slides in connection with your work? If you have not used the feature in the past month put in a zero. Broken out by Gender of survey participant

Gender of survey participant	Mean	Median	Minimum	Maximum
Male	0,00	0,00	0,00	0,00
Female	0,08	0,00	0,00	1,00

Table 5.22.1 Approximately how much time in the past month have you personally spent (in hours or fractions thereof) using Google Groups in connection with your work? If you have not used the feature in the past month put in a zero.

	Mean	Median	Minimum	Maximum
Entire sample	0,24	0,00	0,00	10,00

Table 5.22.2 Approximately how much time in the past month have you personally spent (in hours or fractions thereof) using Google Groups in connection with your work? If you have not used the feature in the past month put in a zero. Broken out by Population size of the area served

Population size of the area served	Mean	Median	Minimum	Maximum
Less than 2000	0,02	0,00	0,00	0,25
2000 - 10000	1,02	0,00	0,00	10,00
10000+ - 45000	0,00	0,00	0,00	0,00
More than 45000	0,04	0,00	0,00	0,50

Table 5.22.3 Approximately how much time in the past month have you personally spent (in hours or fractions thereof) using Google Groups in connection with your work? If you have not used the feature in the past month put in a zero. Broken out by Age range of survey participant

Age range of survey participant	Mean	Median	Minimum	Maximum
Under 30	0,00	0,00	0,00	0,00
30-39	0,04	0,00	0,00	0,25
40-49	1,43	0,00	0,00	10,00
50-59	0,01	0,00	0,00	0,20
60-69	0,06	0,00	0,00	0,50
70 or Over	0,00	0,00	0,00	0,00

Table 5.22.4 Approximately how much time in the past month have you personally spent (in hours or fractions thereof) using Google Groups in connection with your work? If you have not used the feature in the past month put in a zero. Broken out by Library's annual budget, $

Library's annual budget, $	Mean	Median	Minimum	Maximum
Less than 50000	0,02	0,00	0,00	0,25
50000 - 300000	0,00	0,00	0,00	0,00
300000+ - 1500000	0,78	0,00	0,00	10,00
More than 1500000	0,05	0,00	0,00	0,50

Table 5.22.5 Approximately how much time in the past month have you personally spent (in hours or fractions thereof) using Google Groups in connection with your work? If you have not used the feature in the past month put in a zero. Broken out by Gender of survey participant

Gender of survey participant	Mean	Median	Minimum	Maximum
Male	0,00	0,00	0,00	0,00
Female	0,27	0,00	0,00	10,00

Table 5.23.1 Approximately how much time in the past month have you personally spent (in hours or fractions thereof) using Google Analytics in connection with your work? If you have not used the feature in the past month put in a zero.

	Mean	Median	Minimum	Maximum
Entire sample	0,46	0,00	0,00	5,00

Table 5.23.2 Approximately how much time in the past month have you personally spent (in hours or fractions thereof) using Google Analytics in connection with your work? If you have not used the feature in the past month put in a zero. Broken out by Population size of the area served

Population size of the area served	Mean	Median	Minimum	Maximum
Less than 2000	0,09	0,00	0,00	1,00
2000 - 10000	0,41	0,00	0,00	2,00
10000+ - 45000	0,58	0,00	0,00	4,00
More than 45000	0,71	0,00	0,00	5,00

Table 5.23.3 Approximately how much time in the past month have you personally spent (in hours or fractions thereof) using Google Analytics in connection with your work? If you have not used the feature in the past month put in a zero. Broken out by Age range of survey participant

Age range of survey participant	Mean	Median	Minimum	Maximum
Under 30	0,00	0,00	0,00	0,00
30-39	1,17	0,50	0,00	4,00
40-49	1,64	2,00	0,00	5,00
50-59	0,08	0,00	0,00	1,00
60-69	0,13	0,00	0,00	1,00
70 or Over	0,00	0,00	0,00	0,00

Table 5.23.4 Approximately how much time in the past month have you personally spent (in hours or fractions thereof) using Google Analytics in connection with your work? If you have not used the feature in the past month put in a zero. Broken out by Library's annual budget, $

Library's annual budget, $	Mean	Median	Minimum	Maximum
Less than 50000	0,09	0,00	0,00	1,00
50000 - 300000	0,17	0,00	0,00	2,00
300000+ - 1500000	0,55	0,10	0,00	2,00
More than 1500000	1,10	0,00	0,00	5,00

Table 5.23.5 Approximately how much time in the past month have you personally spent (in hours or fractions thereof) using Google Analytics in connection with your work? If you have not used the feature in the past month put in a zero. Broken out by Gender of survey participant

Gender of survey participant	Mean	Median	Minimum	Maximum
Male	1,20	0,00	0,00	4,00
Female	0,37	0,00	0,00	5,00

Table 5.24.1 Approximately how much time in the past month have you personally spent (in hours or fractions thereof) using Blogger in connection with your work? If you have not used the feature in the past month put in a zero.

	Mean	Median	Minimum	Maximum
Entire sample	1,35	0,00	0,00	50,00

Table 5.24.2 Approximately how much time in the past month have you personally spent (in hours or fractions thereof) using Blogger in connection with your work? If you have not used the feature in the past month put in a zero. Broken out by Population size of the area served

Population size of the area served	Mean	Median	Minimum	Maximum
Less than 2000	0,00	0,00	0,00	0,00
2000 - 10000	1,20	0,00	0,00	10,00
10000+ - 45000	3,85	0,00	0,00	50,00
More than 45000	0,00	0,00	0,00	0,00

Table 5.24.3 Approximately how much time in the past month have you personally spent (in hours or fractions thereof) using Blogger in connection with your work? If you have not used the feature in the past month put in a zero. Broken out by Age range of survey participant

Age range of survey participant	Mean	Median	Minimum	Maximum
Under 30	16,67	0,00	0,00	50,00
30-39	0,00	0,00	0,00	0,00
40-49	1,71	0,00	0,00	10,00
50-59	0,00	0,00	0,00	0,00
60-69	0,00	0,00	0,00	0,00
70 or Over	0,00	0,00	0,00	0,00

Table 5.24.4 Approximately how much time in the past month have you personally spent (in hours or fractions thereof) using Blogger in connection with your work? If you have not used the feature in the past month put in a zero. Broken out by Library's annual budget, $

Library's annual budget, $	Mean	Median	Minimum	Maximum
Less than 50000	0,00	0,00	0,00	0,00
50000 - 300000	0,17	0,00	0,00	2,00
300000+ - 1500000	4,62	0,00	0,00	50,00
More than 1500000	0,00	0,00	0,00	0,00

Table 5.24.5 Approximately how much time in the past month have you personally spent (in hours or fractions thereof) using Blogger in connection with your work? If you have not used the feature in the past month put in a zero. Broken out by Gender of survey participant

Gender of survey participant	Mean	Median	Minimum	Maximum
Male	0,00	0,00	0,00	0,00
Female	1,51	0,00	0,00	50,00

Table 5.25.1 Approximately how much time in the past month have you personally spent (in hours or fractions thereof) using YouTube in connection with your work? If you have not used the feature in the past month put in a zero.

	Mean	Median	Minimum	Maximum
Entire sample	3,58	1,00	0,00	30,00

Table 5.25.2 Approximately how much time in the past month have you personally spent (in hours or fractions thereof) using YouTube in connection with your work? If you have not used the feature in the past month put in a zero. Broken out by Population size of the area served

Population size of the area served	Mean	Median	Minimum	Maximum
Less than 2000	4,68	0,50	0,00	20,00
2000 - 10000	2,26	1,00	0,00	10,00
10000+ - 45000	3,02	1,00	0,00	10,00
More than 45000	4,28	1,00	0,00	30,00

Table 5.25.3 Approximately how much time in the past month have you personally spent (in hours or fractions thereof) using YouTube in connection with your work? If you have not used the feature in the past month put in a zero. Broken out by Age range of survey participant

Age range of survey participant	Mean	Median	Minimum	Maximum
Under 30	0,73	1,00	0,20	1,00
30-39	6,50	4,50	0,00	20,00
40-49	1,43	1,00	0,00	5,00
50-59	4,67	1,00	0,00	30,00
60-69	2,91	2,50	0,00	10,00
70 or Over	0,17	0,00	0,00	0,50

Table 5.25.4 Approximately how much time in the past month have you personally spent (in hours or fractions thereof) using YouTube in connection with your work? If you have not used the feature in the past month put in a zero. Broken out by Library's annual budget, $

Library's annual budget, $	Mean	Median	Minimum	Maximum
Less than 50000	8,23	4,00	0,00	30,00
50000 - 300000	3,19	2,00	0,00	10,00
300000+ - 1500000	1,41	0,75	0,00	10,00
More than 1500000	1,77	1,00	0,00	5,00

Table 5.25.5 Approximately how much time in the past month have you personally spent (in hours or fractions thereof) using YouTube in connection with your work? If you have not used the feature in the past month put in a zero. Broken out by Gender of survey participant

Gender of survey participant	Mean	Median	Minimum	Maximum
Male	2,80	0,00	0,00	10,00
Female	3,68	1,00	0,00	30,00

What other apps or features offered by Google but not listed above have you found useful and why?

Less than 2000

1) n/a
2) Photo back up
3) None
4) Game Apps for home but for work, nothing at this point.
5) none
6) NA
7) n/a

2000 - 10000

1) None
2) Keep
3) n/a
4) none
5) Shopper
6) n/a
7) Gmail has allowed swifter communication.
8) none
9) None

10000+ - 45000

1) Android is pretty amazing.
2) sync across devices
3) na
4) None

More than 45000

1) Google News
2) Google Now / Google Reminders in conjunction with Calendar helps alert me when I need to be at a meeting, etc...
3) Ability to sync (or view) my work calendar and my personal calendar in same place.
4) Video search--get stuff not on YouTube Shopping--sometimes patrons want "consumer advice" help
5) I can't think of any others.
6) n/a

Which single Google app or feature has saved you the most time or made you much more productive?

Less than 2000

1) none
2) I am just starting to use Google Chat for online classes. I can see where it might occasionally be useful in my work as well.
3) Google drive
4) Chrome, it's nice to have a reliable browser that can load all websites.
5) Google Images
6) chrome
7) Chrome
8) Gmail
9) google calendar
10) google calendar

2000 - 10000

1) worldcat.org borrowing books from other libraries
2) Drive
3) Groups
4) Chrome
5) none
6) gmail, calendar, maps
7) image search
8) g mail
9) none
10) Gmail & Google Images

10000+ - 45000

1) Google Search
2) Search
3) Drive
4) youtube
5) Calendar and gmail
6) na
7) Google Drive
8) None
9) Google Images
10) G-Mail
11) Google images

More than 45000

1) Google Drive

2) General Google search is of the most use; advanced search when needing more guidance.
3) google search
4) Drive for sure. The ability to share files has become essential
5) Advanced search, with Maps coming in a close second place
6) Google maps
7) Images
8) Gmail
9) Google Drive
10) Google Translate
11) Advanced Search
12) Chrome
13) Google Drive
14) Chrom

If there was one app or feature in Google that you would like to let your peers know about which one would that be.

Less than 2000

1) I don't know
2) Google drive
3) Chrome
4) Google images, or Google Maps
5) chrome
6) Chrome or maps are no brainers--use them all the time.
7) Gmail
8) google drive

2000 - 10000

1) Gmail, Google Images
2) Keep
3) Groups
4) None
5) none
6) maps, calendar
7) advanced search
8) nona
9) Gmail

10000+ - 45000

1) Google Scholar is often overlooked.
2) Sync
3) GoogleBooks
4) calendar
5) na
6) Google+
7) None
8) Googl books

More than 45000

1) Google Drive
2) the ability to easily limit to Australian results
3) Drive for the above reasons
4) None-my colleagues are already quite knowledgeable.
5) Scholar
6) Google Books. Opens up so much information!
7) Google Docs
8) Google Translate

9) Chrome, maps
10) Hangouts

Made in United States
Orlando, FL
04 November 2026

90209254R00122